31 Signposts to Happiness

A Month of Devotional Meditations
on
the Bible's word for
Happiness

Signposts to Happiness
Published by Even Before Publishing;
a division of Wombat Books
P. O. Box 1519, Capalaba Qld 4157
www.evenbeforepublishing.com
www.wombatbooks.com.au

© Ray Hawkins 2014
Design and layout by Even Before Publishing

ISBN: 9781921632730

National Library of Australia Cataloguing-in-Publication entry
Author: Hawkins, Ray, author.
Title: Signpost of happiness / Ray Hawkins.
ISBN: 9781921632730 (paperback)
Subjects: Happiness--Religious aspects--Christianity.
            Happiness--Biblical teaching.
Dewey Number: 248.4

All rights reserved. No part of this publication may be reproduced, stored in, or introduced into a retreival system, or transmitted, in any form, or by any means (electronic, mechanical, photocopying, recording or otherwise) without the prior written permission of the publisher.

Unless otherwise cited, Scripture quotations are taken from the NRSV Reference bible with the apocrypha. Copyright © 1993 by Zondervan Publishing house. All rights reserved.

31 Signposts to Happiness

A Month of Devotional Meditations
on
the Bible's word for
Happiness
by Raymond N Hawkins

Contents

Introduction

Signpost to Happiness   vii

The Book with the Happiness Promise

Day: 1   1

Pathway of Happiness

Day: 2   3

When God Smiles

Day: 3   5

Happiness Comes from being Awestruck

Day: 4   7

Are You Hilarious?

Day: 5   9

Vigilance Protects Happiness

Day: 6   12

How Can the Hungry be Happy?

Day: 7   15

Knowing Your Destination Undergirds Happiness

Day: 8   17

The Might of Meekness

Day: 9   19

The Miracle of Mercy	
Day: 10	21
The Heart of Peacemakers	
Day: 11	23
Persecuted, yet Happy	
Day: 12	25
Happiness in Unknown Territory	
Day: 13	27
The Positives and Negatives for Happiness	
Day: 14	29
Happy are the Poor—Really	
Day: 15	31
Purity of Heart Breeds Happiness	
Day: 16	34
Weeping has a Use-by Date	
Day: 17	36
Is it Ears or Eyes for Happiness?	
Day: 18	38
The Place in which Happiness Abides	
Day: 19	40
The Blessing of Reproof	
Day: 20	42

Enjoying the Second Mile

Day: 21   44

Christ's Enlistment Slogan

Day: 22   46

The Marriage Celebration

Day: 23   48

Cause and Effect

Day: 24   50

Happiness' Enrichment Centre

Day: 25   52

Foundation for Happiness

Day: 26   54

Protected by the Conscience

Day: 27   57

Where Fear and Happiness Embrace

Day: 28   59

The Refreshment of Happiness

Day: 29   61

Death Confronts Happiness

Day: 30   63

Those Whom the Lord Serves

Day: 31   66

Introduction
Signpost to Happiness

My wife and I were driving through the central west of New South Wales. We were off the beaten track and unsure where we were. The weather was cold and wet. Daylight was receding, although there were a few hours left until sunset. That was comforting because we didn't know how far it was to anywhere.

We came to a T intersection. In front of us was a sign leaning precariously. However it was still upright enough to show us both the name of a town and how distant it was. That sign uplifted our weary minds and anxious thoughts with a sense of happiness.

These devotional meditations are designed to be 'Signposts' for travellers engaged in the journey of life. It doesn't matter if you've stuck to the main street, taken a few detours down its side tracks or even got lost in the outback. These directions for happiness come from God's Word and have stood the test for a couple of thousand years.

In most translations of Scripture the word happiness isn't readily found. The word used instead is blessed. That is another way of saying: 'happiness upon happiness' or 'exceedingly happy'.

The Lord's intention for us is to be exceedingly happy, despite the despair of the world around us. Our society is laden with pressures trying to make us miserable or addicted. So much of our culture points to a dead end. The signposts of God have to compete with gaudily painted notices pointing in the opposite direction and promising instant fulfilment.

In Scripture there is also the emphasis on joy. Sometimes we can consider happiness as fleeting and joy as enduring. In the light of how blessed can be translated, maybe we should not make such a distinction. Perhaps we could consider joy as happiness which has gone through the fires of life. On such a journey, we've found God faithful even amidst the tears. Joy may well be happiness in its deeper and more mature dimension, confident in the grace and strength of God's grace.

I pray that as you read the Sign for the day, it will encourage you to take God at His word and begin to travel in the direction it points.

The key verse for this 31–day series is Numbers 6:24–26.

> *The Lord bless you and keep you;*
> *The Lord make His face shine*
> *Upon you and be gracious*
> *Unto you;*
> *The Lord turn His face towards you*
> *And give you peace.*

Raymond N Hawkins

The Book with the Happiness Promise
Day: 1

Key verse: 'Blessed is the one who reads aloud the words of this prophecy, and blessed are those who hear and keep what is written in it; for the time is near.' (Revelation 1:3)

In the days of manuscripts, scrolls and parchments the public reading of Scripture was important. This was true, and still is, where the audience is illiterate. There's an art to reading Scripture out loud for others to understand and digest. The apostle Paul made this clear in 1Timothy 4:13: 'Until I come, devote yourself to the public reading of Scripture, to preaching and to teaching.' Public reading was on a par, if not higher, than preaching or teaching.

Why would John link a sense of personal happiness to the one who reads aloud from Revelation? It may be due to the Holy Spirit using the spoken word to speak to the hearer. In return the reader is blessed and refreshed in his or her own faith. There are seven references to happiness found in Revelation. Each is illuminating in its context. Each displays some aspect of Christ's promise, power and providence.

The promise to the hearer about experiencing happiness from this book is there for the receiving. Unfortunately, between the mouth of the reader and the mind of the hearer can be many distractions or causes of 'deafness'.

In the parable of the sower Jesus highlights three. Matthew 13 has the story. When God's Word is broadcast it lodges in the minds of hearers. One type of mind is hard ground. The person is unconvinced either through poor presentation or from a hardening of the heart. Satan steals it.

Another person is shallow in spiritual knowledge, but nevertheless, the Word takes root, only to shrivel under opposition. The third allows the weeds of worry, affluence and pleasures to strangle it. The person becomes deaf to God's voice, missing out on the wonder of godly happiness through unbelief and distractions. The fourth illustration is that of the prepared mind: the Word lodges in it and grows to bear abundant fruit.

God in His grace continues to give the deaf or distracted other opportunities to hear His Word. He does not abandon His work on the human heart and mind. Still, even those who heard and believed need to be careful. There are outside forces intent on ruining His work by encouraging weeds, dumping rocks or hardening the soil of the heart. This happens through enticing us into disobedience and disbelief. Agents of godlessness use temptation, fear and doubt in an attempt to choke our spiritual fruitfulness.

'We must pay more careful attention therefore, to what we have heard so that we do not drift away.' (Hebrews 2:1)

Happiness cannot be framed and put on the wall as a certificate of merit. To be blessed by God has its high moments of exhilaration and the quieter times of delight. Our defence against a loss of happiness is explained by John in: '… blessed are those who hear and keep what is written …' It's all in the word 'keep'. In the NIV translation it says, 'take it to heart'. The idea suggests a believer should be a watchman on a castle battlement keeping a lookout for enemy infiltration. Our telescope to spot danger is what is written. At the same time God's word is a microscope. We turn it upon our soul's attitudes and behaviour. Are we being true to what is written?

In Revelation John takes us through current and foretold events which threaten the happiness of God's people. This explains why he joins happiness to keeping what is written. Revelation begins with the majesty of Christ and its ability to thrill the hearts of the faithful. Then it presents the judgements of Christ against all that corrupts, oppresses and denies godliness. The book concludes with the glories of Christ's victory and the new heaven and earth.

As we face uncertain times in a turbulent world, the Bible nourishes faith and strengthens hope. It also warns and informs us about coming events. As we read our understanding about God being in control grows. That's happiness.

Today's signpost: 'Behold, I am coming soon! Blessed is he who keeps the words of the prophecy in this book.' (Revelation 22:7)

Pathway of Happiness
Day: 2

Reading: 'Happy are those whose way is blameless, who walk in the Law of the Lord. Happy are those who keep His decrees, who seek Him with their whole heart.' (Psalm 119:1–2)

Psalm 119 is a majestic psalm about the benefits of saturating yourself in God's Word. It is a masterpiece woven out of personal experience from youthfulness to old age. The psalms take us through good times and much hardship. We have the testimony of both the old and new covenants and therefore have so much more reason to grasp God's Word. We would be wise to copy the example of verse 11: 'I treasure Your word in my heart so that I might not sin against You.' We need to hide it in our hearts so it will guide our steps and strengthen our spiritual stamina.

In the opening verse we are confronted by a bold claim about finding, knowing and staying happy. It isn't an oasis where we can retreat or a prescription we should take. Rather, happiness is a journey in fellowship with the law, precepts, statutes and commands of God.

Then the man of faith cries out: 'Oh, that my ways may be steadfast in keeping Your statutes.' (Psalm119:5) He's realised our wayward hearts derail our good intentions. Such detours lead our feet astray or make commitment feeble. When we stray, we are no longer blameless. Happiness shrinks or even evaporates. It's replaced by guilt and shame. In verse 9 he raises a question that affects us all: 'How can young people keep their way pure?' The answer from the same verse is: 'By guarding it according to Your word.'

How easy to write. How hard to be consistent. The pathway which we walk with happiness is strewn with dangers, snares and opponents. We are not always successful in avoiding them. However, verse 26 tells us: 'When I told of my ways, You answered me; teach me Your statutes.'

How did he give an account? Undoubtedly on his knees! How wonderful that he felt free to approach the Lord after taking wrong turns or going up dead ends. 'I implore Your favour with all my heart; be gracious to me according to Your promise. When I think on Your ways, I turn my feet to Your decrees.' (verses 58–59)

The idea behind 'turn' is either the call to repentance or the act of doing it. The way of happiness doesn't mean we travel it without scars. They become signs of God's healing grace from the wounds of our self–will and ignorance. Surely we can say amen to verse 29: 'Put false ways far from me; and graciously teach me Your law.'

Some interesting words are used in verses 30–35: they are 'chosen', 'cling', 'run', 'teach', 'give' and 'lead'. Each one seems to be an act of the person's will. How important is this for us? The Christian faith isn't fatalistic. Nor is it pacifistic. God calls and we must respond. He provides. He also expects us to go the 'storeroom' and receive that which we need. Where is that? In His law, statutes, precepts and commands. When spiritual laziness or ineptitude reigns, there is no energy to fulfil those action and words. Misery, not happiness, is the road then travelled.

We have already noticed our responsibility in returning to the pathway of happiness. What is the psalmist's promise offered from out of his own discovery? Psalm119:165: 'Great peace have those who love Your law, nothing can make them stumble.'

Each one of us will tread a different trail in our life of discipleship. However, within the individual heart there is only one pathway to enjoy happiness. It begins and culminates in the Lord Jesus who said if we abide in His word we will have peace. That emotional and spiritual security is the travelling companion of happiness.

Today's signpost: 'Your word is a lamp to my feet and a light to my path. I have sworn an oath and confirmed it, to observe your righteous ordinances.' (Psalm 119:105–106)

When God Smiles

Day: 3

Key verse: 'The Lord bless you and keep you; the Lord make His face to shine upon you and be gracious to you; the Lord lift up His countenance upon you, and give you peace.' (Numbers 6:24–26)

How would you describe a smile? What does it do to the face of a person? What effect does it have on the recipient? My dictionary says a smile is 'to look pleased, show pleasure, favour and kindness.'

The verse quoted above seems to me to equate the shine on God's face with the smile of His favour. You will notice also the doctrine of the Godhead, Father, Son, Holy Spirit, is embraced in the three–fold use of 'Lord'. God ordained the priestly blessing upon His pilgrim people to assure them of His favour. When they journeyed under such a blessing they knew the secret of happiness. The same applies to us today. Happiness is only sustainable in daily life under the smile of God. Therefore the longing of the heart is found not in things or accomplishments. It is linked to God's smile.

God is unseen by our eyes yet He is known in our spirits. We may not hear His voice yet we have His written word. Therefore it is possible for us to live under the glow of God's face as He watches over us. How? Through knowing and obeying His Word as it grabs our heart, challenges our mind and increases our faith.

The psalmists repeatedly talk about desiring and experiencing the smile of God shining upon them. Their sense of this happiness is tied in with a quality of life pleasing to the Lord. Such a quality is called righteousness. What does this mean? Living in accordance with the spiritual, moral, ethical requirements of God.

Unfortunately, there is the constant danger our behaviour will force God to look away. Isaiah 59:1–2: 'See, the Lord's hand is not too short to save, nor His ear too dull to hear. Rather, your iniquities have been barriers between you and your God, and your sins have hidden His face from you, so that He does not hear you.'

The history of Israel and the Church bears out this tragedy. Psalm 34:16: 'the face of the Lord is against evildoers'. It is terrible to the soul when we sense God is not smiling at us. Much more fearsome however is when God turns an unsmiling face towards those who continue in their unrepentant way. Happiness then is impossible!

When the Lord looks at us and knows our heart is set on Him we bring delight to Him. His joy in us expresses itself in blessings. This is regardless of the circumstances in which we find ourselves. Many testify to knowing the pleasure of the Lord in the midst of aggressive atheism, antipathy or aloneness. Such happiness defies explanation, apart from God's promise that he will be active in the believer's heart.

King David of Israel wrote Psalm 3. In it we note his struggles. Read it in its entirety and note his honesty before the Lord. As the king he was expected to read portions of the Law of Moses daily (Deuteronomy 17:18–19). His familiarity with our key verse is evident throughout his writings. 'But trust in You, O Lord; I say, "You are my God". My times are in Your hand; deliver me from the hand of my enemies and persecutors. Let Your face shine on your servant; save me in Your steadfast love.' (Psalm 31:14–16)

As Christians we look forward to the time when we shall see our Lord 'face to face'. What a wonderful, awe–inspiring time that will be. No words can adequately express the wonder that will then fill our hearts. Until then we are to walk by faith in accordance with His Word. Then we will know His face is shining upon us. It is said that when Moses met with the Lord and came down from the mountain his face shone. It is similar for us. Whenever we meet with our Lord and are faithful in our calling His beauty is reflected without our knowing. (2 Corinthians 3:18)

Today's signpost: 'For it is the God who said, "Let light shine out of darkness", who has shone in our hearts to give the light of the knowledge of the glory of God in the face of Jesus Christ.' (2 Corinthians 4:6)

Happiness Comes from being Awestruck
Day: 4

Key verse: 'Happy is everyone who fears the Lord, who walks in His ways.' (Psalm 128:1)

Happiness and fear at first glance appear incompatible. To our mind 'fear' has a negative, scary image, something far removed from happiness. As with many words, there are shades of meaning woven into one expression. Depending upon the context fear can mean being 'awestruck or reverent' or 'frightened or cowered'.

The Bible seeks to reveal the Lord God in His majesty and mystery. This would make us tremble at His holiness and fear for our well being. The Scriptures also reveal the Lord as the One who cares for us, loves us and shows the way into His heart. The fear which crushes is transformed by grace into awe and reverence. When the apostle Paul wrote to the Corinthians he reminded them of the father–child relationship. We enjoy this by faith in Jesus Christ. Because of that relationship he says, 'let us cleanse ourselves from every defilement of body and of spirit, making holiness perfect in the fear of God.' (2 Corinthians 7:1)

How is it possible for us to maintain our sense of awe in a world of unbelief?

Israel was on the edge of crossing into the Promised Land. Waiting for them were the 'giants' their forefathers would not confront. To defeat idolatry, fierce opposition and seductive faith–destroying pleasures needed more than determination. Moses outlined some important strategies in Deuteronomy 31:12–13: 'Assemble the people—men, women and children as well as the aliens residing in your towns—so that they may hear and learn to fear the Lord your God and to observe diligently, all the words of this law, and so that their children, who have not known it, may hear and learn to fear the Lord your God, as long as you live in the land you are crossing over the Jordan to possess.'

Did you latch onto those four key words Moses used to emphasise how to maintain the awe? We live in different circumstances, yet the principles of those four words remain as fresh and important as ever.

Assemble is the first word in maintaining the awe. You and I need to assemble with those of similar mind to encourage each other's faith. Bearing testimony to God's faithful dealings helps us to hang in there through our personal hard times. The awesomeness of God's mercy is felt when a man or woman tells of God's forgiveness. Psalm 130:3: 'If You, O Lord, should mark iniquities, Lord, who could stand? But there is forgiveness with You, so that You may be revered.'

Hear is the reason for getting together. It is more than mere listening. It means to inwardly digest what is said and take it to heart. Listening requires a receptive spirit and a desire to understand. What you listen to can make a positive or negative contribution to your happiness. When you come together for worship and teaching you need to hear the Word of God. As Paul reminded Titus: 'Teach what is consistent with sound doctrine.' (Titus 2:1)

Learn is not passive, it is active. It means putting into practice what you have been taught. Those called to be preachers/teachers will be required to account before God for what they teach. Hearers have a similar accountability to discern, then apply, what is being taught. The purpose of learning is to make us walk according to the will and ways of the Lord.

Observe the way of the Lord. We are not called to be daydreamers, wishful thinkers or theorists. Happiness is fed and enriched by discovering new dimensions to life, to self and to God's delight in us. Israel had to cross over into the land to inherit their blessing. We must also leave past failures, apathy and self–indulgence behind to inherit God's happiness. Jesus made 'follow' a key word when inviting people to enjoy His happiness. You will find the blessing of God fades the longer you remain immobilised from following His teachings. Fear which motivates is the handmaiden to happiness! That's awesome!

Today's signpost: 'The Lord takes pleasure in those who fear Him, in those who hope in His steadfast love.' (Psalm 147:11)

Are You Hilarious?
Day: 5

Key verse: 'It is more blessed to give than to receive.' (Acts 20:35)

Scrooge in Charles Dickens' novel *A Christmas Carol* is the classic example of one who hoarded wealth. However, it didn't make him happy. He was beset by misery and loneliness. His transformation after he is confronted by his past, present and future makes for interesting reading. The reality of what happened was depicted by his generosity to the family of Tiny Tim.

Happiness isn't something which can be stored. There is something lively about it. In the key verse this liveliness is defined as giving. In the verse's context the apostle Paul uses himself as an example of someone experiencing happiness. On the surface his outline, both here and elsewhere, seems rather strange, to say the least. He mentions imprisonment, persecution, disappointments and tears in his ministry. When he ends with the quote by Jesus, the hearers' jaws must have dropped open. Paul was insisting that despite what he had come through he was enjoying heaven's happiness.

Christians are on a journey to discover Christ's promised happiness. The unforgettable statement of John 3:16: 'For God so loved the world that He gave His own Son …' confronts us with the God who gives. By implication this means God is the Lord of happiness. He gives and gives and gives. We receive it and call it grace. I wonder if the Almighty would name it as a source of His happiness. From the first chapters of Genesis we discover His pleasure in giving. The Lord God provided Adam with Eve and also with the Garden of Eden as a dwelling. Even when they had violated His command God provided them with clothing. Scripture is permeated by insights into the God who enjoys giving, especially to His battling servants.

When we respond to God's mercy we experience Romans 6:23: 'The free gift of God is eternal life in Christ Jesus our Lord.' How then does this life work itself out as a result of this giving? I'm sure the first thing that comes to mind is dollars and cents. This is true in part, but it isn't the whole story. 2 Corinthians 9:7 says, 'Each of you must give as you have made up your mind, not reluctantly or under compulsion, for God loves a cheerful giver.' There is that readiness of mind, a joyousness of gratitude which motivates. The English word hilarious stems from the Greek word for cheerful. I wonder how many times we have felt hilarious as we have presented our gifts in the name of our Lord God!

The idea of giving encompasses so much more than money. Read Paul's letter to Philemon. It contains a challenge to the owner of a runaway slave to offer forgiveness when the fugitive returns. Imagine how costly such an act would be. How would the pagan owners of other slaves view it? Forgiveness is the gift we offer to others who have hurt us. It's in the giving we know the joy of heaven. The forgiven will only enjoy it if they repent.

Another aspect of happiness through giving is mentioned in Hebrews 13:2. 'Do not neglect to show hospitality to strangers, for by doing that some have entertained angels without knowing it'. Hospitality doesn't mean a lavish spread. It is sharing what you have as a mark of respect. It is meeting the need of another. The pleasure received in the unsettling of the daily routine is summed up in the possibility of entertaining 'angels' unknowingly.

We all know of people with wonderful ability with their hands. In Acts 9:39 we hear: 'A disciple whose name was Tabitha ... was devoted to good works and acts of charity.' She had a giving heart and expressed it through her ability. Have we had someone come to our aid to fix a problem by their expertise without cost? What a humbling yet lovely act to receive a food parcel by neighbours in our time of need. Their giving becomes a blessing to both the giver and the receiver.

We must guard against a monster hiding in our soul and wanting to corrupt the happiness of giving. It believes in letting not only the left hand know what the right hand has done but also everyone else as well. To keep it under control we are instructed to do as much as we can in secret or unpublicised. Matthew 6:1.4 tells us: 'Beware of practicing your piety before others in order to be seen by them … your alms … done in secret … your Father who sees in secret will reward you.'

Today's signpost: 'All day long the wicked covet, but the righteous give and do not hold back.' (Proverbs 21:26)

Vigilance Protects Happiness
Day: 6

Key verse: 'See, I am coming like a thief! Blessed is the one who stays awake and is clothed, not going about naked and exposed to shame.' (Revelation 16:15)

Physical sleep is vital to health, however to go to sleep spiritually is dangerous. Ultimately, it becomes embarrassing as we stand before the Lord. Throughout the Gospels and the letters these words echo: 'Sleeper, awake! Rise from the dead, and Christ will shine on you.' (Ephesians 5:14)

What puts our spiritual life to sleep?

The wine of Babylon! What is such a drink? It's a potent mixture brewed by the powers of darkness lavishly offered in the World. When tasted it is totally addictive and poisonous to godliness and personal happiness. What are the ingredients which cause a stupor of the mind and paralysis of the spirit? John describes the contents of the cup in Revelation. They are summed up as idolatry, occultic influences, immorality and affluence. For disciples of Christ the wine of Babylon befuddles faith, godliness, truth and spiritual motivation. Happiness requires abstinence. Only then can we guard against sipping oneself into lethargy, laziness and loss of honour.

How then can we stay awake and resist the enticing invitation to sit and sip? Recognise the enemy's intention and understanding the danger posed. The warning signs are not on the cup. They are in God's word. Is it any wonder that the wine merchants of Babylon don't want you to read and study the Scriptures!

1 Peter 5:8–9: 'Discipline yourselves, keep alert. Like a roaring lion your adversary the devil prowls around, looking for someone to devour. Resist him, steadfast in your faith …' When you are under the wine's influence you are easy prey to its 'brewer'—the devil. There isn't any happiness in hell.

The key verse likens Jesus' return to judge and rule as the coming of a thief in the night. It is unheralded. It is not unexpected by those who believe His teachings. No day or hour has been made known, only the fact of His return. We may well enter His presence long before what is revealed happens. However, the truth of being spiritually awake and happy—or asleep and ashamed—applies. 'So whether we are at home or away, we make it our aim to please Him. For all of us must appear before the judgement seat of Christ, so that each may receive recompense for what has been done in the body, whether good or evil.' (2 Corinthians 5:9–10)

Why does the Lord insist happiness requires being awake and keeping one's clothes on? It points us back to Genesis 3. Adam sinned against God. Adam and Eve realised their nakedness and were ashamed. God clothed them in the skin of an animal, probably a sheep. Sin also made us naked, unclean and spiritually dead in God's sight. When He redeemed us, He also clothed us in Christ's righteousness.

The wine of Babylon aims to make us forget or disrobe from our spiritual clothing. This exposes us to moral and spiritual sleeping sickness. In turn we are held up to ridicule and hypocrisy. Our spiritual nakedness and ungodly living rebounds upon Jesus Christ. He is made an object of mockery.

To resist the cup of Babylonian wine may result in various forms of harassment and rejection. The one thing it cannot do, however, is steal your God–ordained happiness. This sense of wellbeing is reinforced by the knowledge of Babylon's judgement. Revelation 18 highlights that fact, which is yet to occur. It will happen. Although the event is in the future this principle is always current: 'Come out of her, My people, so that you do not take part in her sins, and so that you do not share in her plagues … She will be burned with fire; for mighty is the Lord God who judges her.'

Happiness has no hangover. Its nectar is called the cup of blessing. It is the wine of salvation formulated by Jesus Christ at Calvary. Every time a person celebrates with that cup something happens. The reality of happiness deepens while the wonder of love increases. The radiance of Christ's garment of righteousness over us also glows brighter! Surely we can join with the Psalmist to say: 'What shall I return to the Lord for all His bounty to me? I will lift up the cup of salvation and call on the name of the Lord, I will pay my vows to the Lord in the presence of all His people.' (Psalm 116:12–14)

Today's signpost: 'Keep alert stand firm in your faith, be courageous, be strong.' (1 Corinthians 16:13)

How Can the Hungry be Happy?
Day: 7

Key verse: 'Blessed are you who are hungry now, for you will be filled.' (Luke 6:21)

There isn't much fun in being famished. The agony of hunger is compounded by the aroma of food denied to the starving. Disciples of Christ have and will endure such torment as hunger, thirst, scorching heat and tears, especially in the great tribulation. (Revelation 7:14–17) What sustains a person's faith, hope and love in the Lord Jesus under such unwarranted circumstances?

A casual glance at Luke's account would leave us with the impression that the hungry person will be filled. There isn't any mention of their spiritual relationship with God. However Luke has strategically framed his words. They come between Jesus' statement about the Kingdom of God and enduring all for the sake of the Son of Man.

In the crowd there would have been those with a knowledge of the prophets. When they listened to Jesus, did Isaiah 49:8–10 come to mind? 'Thus says the Lord: In a time of favour I have answered you, on a day of salvation I have helped you …They shall not hunger nor thirst, neither scorching wind nor sun shall strike them down, for He who has pity on them will lead them, and by springs of water will guide them.' Was Jesus implying the acceptable year of the Lord was casting its rays of light right at that time?

Jesus looked at His listeners and understood their individual situations. If He was seeking popular endorsement how easy it would have been to turn stones into bread and leaves into coins. However, what good would such transient acts do in the long term for them and for future generations? The Lord who knew hunger, tears and poverty called His disciples to walk with Him into the promised Kingdom. The destination is sure. The journey, however, can cover rough and unpleasant ground. Jesus never hides the stark truth involved in being His disciple. The cross as an emblem of discipleship underscores that fact.

Not every believer in Jesus is hungry or poor. However, as a consequence, the fortunate ones have a great responsibility. Isaiah 58:6–8 says, 'Is not this the fast that I choose: to loose the bonds of injustice, to undo the thongs of the yoke, to let the oppressed go free and break every yoke? Is it not to share your bread with the hungry and bring the homeless poor to your house; when you see the naked, to cover them, and not to hide yourself from your own kin?'

This is further underlined by the parable recorded in Matthew 25 about the sheep and the goats. Whilst the parable is actually dealing with nations, the principle for individuals is still relevant. When we do it to those in need we are actually ministering to our Lord. We cannot feed all the hungry or clothe all the naked. We can, however, share our 'widow's coin' (Luke 21:1–4) and be humbled by the pleasure it gives to God as He multiplies it.

The Church, when its heart is in tune with its Lord, lives out the principle of caring for others. 1 John 3:16–17 tells us: 'We know love by this, that He laid down His life for us—and we ought to lay down our lives for one another. How does God's love abide in anyone who has this world's goods and sees a brother or sister in need and yet refuses to help?'

We can only know true happiness, whether rich or poor, hungry or full, from an unbreakable assurance. Such a confidence which guarantees God's coming kingdom is found in Jesus. As we face the uncertainties of our everyday we can have an abiding confidence. Read what held Habakkuk together in the trauma of his day.

Today's signpost: 'Though the fig tree does not blossom, and no fruit is on the vines; though the produce of the olive fails and the fields yield no food; though the flock is cut off from the fold and there is no herd in the stalls, yet I will rejoice in the Lord; I will exult in the God of my Salvation.' (Habakkuk 3:17–18)

Knowing Your Destination Undergirds Happiness
Day: 8

Key verse: 'Blessed and holy are those who share in the first resurrection. Over these the second death has no power, but they will be priests of God and of Christ and they will reign with Him for a thousand years.' (Revelation 20:6)

A burial ground in ancient times was called a 'necropolis'. In the Greek language this means 'city of the dead'. When the gospel of Jesus Christ took hold of a community the name was changed. This time the word became 'cemetery' and means 'a sleeping room'. What a dramatic shift in understanding. If the dead person is sleeping, then it means there will be a waking up time in the future.

The Bible is specific when it talks about that great getting–up time. There are many references in the New Testament to it. Our personal happiness in time and for eternity hinges upon whether or not we are included in the first event! There is no need to be uncertain about your inclusion. The gospel of John includes details about the death and resuscitation of Lazarus. Jesus takes the opportunity to teach about the event highlighted in our key verse. He told Martha, Lazarus' sister, 'I am the resurrection and the life. He who believes in Me will live, even though he dies; and whoever lives and believes in Me will never die. Do you believe this?' (John 11:25) The reference to never dying refers to the second death which is separation from the presence of God.

According to 2 Corinthians 5, when a believer dies he or she enters into the presence of the Lord. Their bodies, however, remain buried. In the mind of God the person's bodily DNA is sleeping, waiting for the trumpet to sound. There is also the loud voice when the dead in Christ will rise and meet the Lord in the air. (1 Thessalonians 4:13–18) When that takes place those sleeping in the dust or in the waters of earth will rise. In the twinkling of an eye we will be transformed. A new destiny required a new body as explained by the apostle Paul. Philippians 3:20–21: 'Our citizenship is in heaven. And it is from there we are expecting a Saviour, the Lord Jesus Christ. He will transform the body of our humiliation that it may conform to the body of His glory by the power that also enables Him to make all things subject to Himself.'

Here again God expresses His desire for us to know the power of happiness. The face of death cannot dint or dull it. The first resurrection guaranteed to us through our union with Christ Jesus declares Christ's triumph in our lives. This is why we are not held hostage by the fear of death. The earth–shattering heaven–opening cry of Easter Sunday morning is our guarantee: 'He is not here; He is risen'!

Holiness is a partner with happiness; indeed, they are inseparable. An unholy person will never know *happiness* as intended by God. Guilt, shame, fear and accountability before God's holy presence will destroy any sense of joy! Those sharing in the first resurrection have been made holy. How? Through Christ at Calvary! He cleansed us from our empty way of life. Peter tells us we inherited emptiness from our Gentile forefathers. Holiness builds into our life protective barriers against any counter–attack by our past.

Our destination also means we are to become priests to minister before God. We think of this confined to heaven. The Lord's Prayer points also to a time on this earth: 'Our Father in heaven, hallowed be Your name, Your kingdom come, Your will be done on earth as it is in heaven.' Imagine that. What an awesome privilege to crown our inclusion in the first resurrection. Can we boast about it? Definitely not! Our boasting can only be in knowing Jesus Christ as our Lord and Saviour.

Today's signpost: 'The Lord Himself, with a cry of command, with the archangel's call and with the sound of God's trumpet, will descend from heaven and the dead in Christ will rise first. Then we who are alive, who are left, will be caught up in the clouds together with them to meet the Lord in the air; and so we will be with the Lord forever.' (1 Thessalonians 4:16–17)

The Might of Meekness
Day: 9

Key verse: 'Blessed are the meek, for they will inherit the earth.' (Matthew 5:5)

Meekness and gentleness are twins—not identical, but very similar. You will often find them together in the New Testament. They express different aspects of character. To my mind, meekness is a captivating expression of a person's soul. I picture a thunderous waterfall, strong, vibrant and inspiring. Gentleness, on the other hand, is the outward action of meekness. It has harnessed the power of meekness and channelled it into tender words and actions.

Two men in Scripture, separated by approximately fourteen hundred years, epitomise these characteristics. Neither Moses in the Old Testament nor Paul in the New would have been considered 'meek men' in their early years. Nor were their actions initially gentle. Moses was a Hebrew adopted just after birth into Pharaoh's court. There he grew up in the culture and learning of the ruling class. However, he never forgot his Hebrew roots. One day, in anger, he killed an Egyptian taskmaster who was ill–treating a Hebrew slave. He tried to bury the evidence. He fled when he was found out. A well–intentioned murderer became dispirited in the wilderness of Midian.

Paul, in his zeal for the Law and his religious heritage, assaulted the Christians. He imprisoned and killed them. In his later testimony he stated he was a blasphemer, persecutor and violent unbeliever. However, Paul was to write and express the essence of meekness. He, Moses and many others across history were men of strong passion, ideals and a sense of their own rightness. Their souls were filled with raging emotional waters cascading unchecked over a mountainous cliff. What changed them? An encounter with the God of Abraham, Isaac and Jacob! He is Yahweh of the Old Testament, Jesus the Christ in the New.

What the Holy Spirit did in their lives is the same thing He does in various ways and measures in everyone He indwells. Before conversion our inner lives are self–centred, self–righteous and self–destructive. It is an unseen, uncontrolled river of passion, pride and prejudice. When we surrender our lives to the Lord Jesus, He begins a major make–over. The passion's flow is cleansed, harnessed and utilised. From this He creates good works with acts of kindness. The statesman of Israel is described in Numbers 12:3: 'Moses was very humble, more so than anyone else on the face of the earth.' Humility expresses meekness. When you read the Scriptures you discover him to be a commander—resolute, compassionate, strong on justice and keen for mercy. Whoever said meekness was weakness never read Moses' life story.

Paul's fiery temper was harnessed by the grace of God. This man would not take a step back from defending the Truth. Undergirding this was a shepherd's heart. 2 Corinthians 10:1:'I myself, Paul, appeal to you by the meekness and gentleness of Christ.'

Jesus mentioned the meek and said they would inherit the world. Certain Scriptures were behind such a statement. The conviction of the psalmist is forthright and clear: Psalm 37:11:'The meek shall inherit the land and delight themselves in abundant prosperity.' This is specifically referring to the promised land of Israel. What the people of Jesus' day saw was the roughshod military shoes of the Roman conquerors. Israel was crushed underfoot. Jesus was saying such conditions are temporary. God's promise is real and eternal. Psalm 149:4:'The Lord takes pleasure in His people; He adorns the humble with victory.' Oh, for such an adorning to take place soon!

Happiness for the meek is due to the fact their surging river of passion, pride, conviction, has been cleansed and harnessed by Christ. Their sanctified temperament brings life and hope, not fear and destruction in its wake. When Jesus said such people will inherit the earth it points to a gift, not a right. As they walk their salvation experience they wait the promises of Christ Jesus.

Today's signpost: 'Seek the Lord all you meek of the earth, who have upheld His justice. Seek righteousness, seek humility. It may be that you will be hidden in the day of the Lord's anger.' (Zephaniah 2:3 NKJV)

The Miracle of Mercy
Day: 10

Key verse: 'Blessed are the merciful, for they will receive mercy.' (Matthew 5:7)

'Go tell that to the religious leaders. And don't forget the Roman governor!' Such may well have been the unspoken words of the crowd listening to Jesus. Mercy, kindness, compassion were acts rarely experienced by the common folk. Towards the end of His earthly ministry Jesus also unmasked the harshness of the religious leaders. With deep sorrow He lamented in Matthew 23:23: 'Woe to you, scribes and Pharisees, hypocrites! For you tithe mint, dill and cummin, and have neglected the weightier matters of the law; justice and mercy and faith.' The sorrow of Jesus would be still keen as those three factors remain neglected and hard to find.

In word and by example Jesus lived out mercy. Why were so many blind to His example and teaching? Probably, among other factors, the expectation of wanting to receive it overrode their willingness to give it. Jesus tried to reverse this approach. Happiness would be theirs if they were proactive even to the ungrateful and the arrogant.

Mercy does not cancel out justice. It doesn't silence judgement. What it does do is soften the full extent of the verdict. The Old Testament describes Yahweh as merciful and just. In Deuteronomy 28 He wrote into His Word that obedience would bring blessing, disobedience would bring beltings. However, Yahweh would never forget His promise and covenant. That is why after the nation's overthrow by Babylon, Jeremiah would write Lamentations 3:22–23: 'The steadfast love of the Lord never ceases, His mercies never come to an end; they are new every morning; great is Your faithfulness.' The baby of Bethlehem reveals the depth of that mercy to the nation.

To a psychologist, mercy may have complex motives. Jesus understood as much when He added, 'for they will be shown mercy'. Who knows when such a time of need may come, either from man or from God? We may not always receive it from friend or foe. From God who understands us, however, mercy waits to wash over us at the moment of our request. Ephesians 2:4–5 says, 'God, who is rich in mercy, out of the great love with which He loved us even when we were dead through our trespasses, made us alive together with Christ—by grace you have been saved.' As you read the rest of the letter it is clear to receive mercy means we extend it to others. Such expressions of compassion may not always be appreciated or understood. People may take it, abuse it, misunderstand it or consider it a weakness. Where's the happiness in that for us? It's twofold. The Spirit of Christ within rejoices in our behaviour and the Father's glory in enhanced.

The small but significant letter of Jude should be read to understand the religious scene today. In it are outlined leaders of apostasy and the emotional turmoil believers will endure. How can we be merciful in a corrupt, selfish and idolatrous society? Briefly, let's walk through some verses from Jude for some clues.

Jude 1:20 says, 'Beloved, build yourselves up on your most holy faith; pray in the Holy Spirit.' The idea is to construct your life on the foundation of grace in Christ. This makes you morally and spiritually earthquake and tsunami–proof. God has supplied the materials. You must construct your life according to His plans.

Jude 1:21 goes on, 'Keep yourselves in love of God; look forward to the mercy of our Lord Jesus Christ that leads to eternal life.' The word picture of 'keep' is to guard, to preserve and to watch over. The world wants to make us forget God's love and mercy. We must be active in remembering, enjoying and expressing it.

Jude 1:22–23 then says, 'Have mercy on some who are wavering; save others by snatching them out of the fire; and have mercy on still others with fear, hating even the tunic defiled by their bodies.' Because Jesus Christ has been kind to us, we, from that relationship, reach out to others. This is the result of verse 20 constantly refreshed by verse 21.

Today's signpost: 'He has told you, O mortal, what is good; and what does the Lord require of you but to do justice, and to love kindness, and to walk humbly with your God.' (Micah 6:8)

The Heart of Peacemakers
Day: 11

Key verse: 'Blessed are the peacemakers, for they will be called children of God.' (Matthew 5:9)

Huge amounts of money, masses of armed forces and harsh penalties are directed towards the maintenance of so–called peace around the world. Such actions should be more correctly termed 'keeping people subdued'. Being a 'peacemaker' is more than subduing people. It is meant to achieve reconciliation, harmony and freedom. This is only possible through righteousness and justice.

In Matthew's account of the Beatitudes, 'peacemakers' is number seven. That is a special number in Scripture which you can check out at your leisure. Is this Beatitude randomly or deliberately locked in at that spot? If you believe nothing is random with the Holy Spirit, then there is some significant implication for us to understand. The clue could well be in the concluding words of the verse: 'called children of God'.

The Son of God, the Lord Jesus, is the Peacemaker. He is called the Prince of Peace (Isaiah 9:6). He is the One who makes peace between individuals and God. Jesus will make peace between tribe and tribe and, one day, between Israel and the nations. Therefore to be called 'children of God' in Matthew's context is to walk in the sandals of Jesus Christ. The intention would be to bring warring factions together in reconciliation. Such noble attempts are not always welcomed, nor are they cost–free.

To be a happy peacemaker requires a person to enjoy being at peace with God. 'Therefore, since we are justified by faith, we have peace with God through our Lord Jesus Christ.' (Romans 5:1) This theme of restoring people to a peace relationship with God is found throughout the New Testament letters. Once established, it spreads to other faith–family members. The power of the cross for salvation is also the motivation for reconciliation. 2 Corinthians 5:18 tells us: 'God, who reconciled us to Himself through

Christ, and has given us the ministry of reconciliation.' Paul was acting as a peacemaker between members of the Church who had taken various factional positions and misused the communion time. His basis for peace and unity stemmed from Christ's mercy.

In the letter to the Philippians, the apostle urges the man he called 'loyal yokefellow' to help two women of faith to settle their disagreement (Philippians 4:2). As you read his other letters, you will find time and again the attitude of Christ the Peacemaker. The Church always stands in need of peacemakers.

To be a peacemaker requires more than pious phrases. There are times when making peace demands rebuke with gentleness. It may mean exposure and prohibition from communion until the issues are resolved. How then does such a mediator of grace and accountability find happiness in his or her role? I think it is self–evident. Seeing lives restored, relationships healed, the congregation enjoying one–mindedness sums it up.

Happiness is walking in the footsteps of Jesus. The apostles undertook this demanding role of peacemakers. We are to follow their lead. There is only one way any of us will be able to do this. That is by being at peace with God and each other through the embrace of Jesus Christ.

Today's signpost: 'A harvest of righteousness is sown in peace for those who make peace.' (James 3:18)

Persecuted, yet Happy
Day: 12

Key verse: 'Blessed are those who are persecuted for righteousness' sake, for theirs is the kingdom of heaven.' (Matthew 5:10)

Jesus must have been the happiest man on earth, according to His own words. He was insulted, opposed, ridiculed for what He said and did. John 5:18: 'For this reason the Jews were seeking all the more to kill Him, because He was not only breaking the Sabbath, but was also calling God His own father, therefore making Himself equal with God.' Ultimately the Romans pulverised His body with their whip, then crucified Him.

How did He react? He prayed for them!

This is the example as well as the teaching Jesus left His disciples. Matthew 5:44: 'Love your enemies and pray for those who persecute you, so that you may be children of your Father in heaven.' The word 'persecute' has the forensic significance of being falsely accused in Luke 6:28. A similar expression is in 1 Peter 3:16: 'Keep your conscience clear, so that when you are maligned, those who abuse you for your good conduct in Christ may be put to shame.'

Persecution and vilification know no boundaries. Nor do they respect any religion. Persecution infects and affects all races and often family relationships. The causes may be many yet they all stem from what Jeremiah calls a deceitful heart, which is beyond cure and impossible to understand. (Jeremiah 17:9)

Followers of Jesus will experience persecution in some form or other for any number of reasons. However, the Lord links a particular sense of happiness to a believer's encounter with opposition. Four dimensions are highlighted: for righteousness, by being falsely accused, for having all kinds of evil said against them and being insulted about the Faith. On what grounds are these things made? 'Because of Me,' said Jesus.

What does Jesus call His disciples to do? Rejoice and be glad!

Don't you think that's a strange solution to being harassed, chased, expelled, denied justice and even killed? Why would anyone rejoice under such circumstances? Because the Lord said they are in the same company as the prophets of God!

Anyone who thinks this behaviour easy hasn't experienced the spirit–crushing effects of the tongue, the lash or banishment. How can a Christian be happy under such a moral, spiritual or physical opposition? Jesus said more about the happiness of the persecuted than those in the other categories of being blessed. Why? Persecution in some form will dominate the lives of His people. 2 Timothy 3:12: 'Indeed, all who want to live a godly life in Christ Jesus will be persecuted.' The Lord empowers happiness with the two fold promise of sharing in the kingdom of heaven and receiving a great reward in heaven. It may not stop the tears. It does counterbalance the tendency to self–pity and negativity when things are tough.

The apostle Peter gave a positive insight about persecution when it happened because a disciple was 'doing good'. How can that make a person feel better? Only by the fact it places you in the same league as Jesus. He expressed goodness in word and deed. Therefore, if Jesus was the happiest man on the planet, let's be infected by some of His happiness.

Today's signpost: 'When reviled, we bless; when persecuted, we endure; when slandered, we speak kindly.' (1 Corinthians 4:12–13)

Happiness in Unknown Territory
Day: 13

Key verse: 'By faith, Abraham obeyed when he was called to set out for a place that he was to receive as an inheritance; and he set out, not knowing where he was going.' (Hebrews 11:8)

Genesis is the book of beginnings. It also has some special words whose use becomes a framework for understanding them in later contexts. The first mention of the word 'blessed' was when God created Adam and Eve! He gave them the grace of His happiness as individuals. God blessed their marital relationship in the same manner as told in Genesis 1:22 and 28. God's desire is for people to know the happiness He offers.

An act of treason demolished the essence of happiness—the spiritual relationship with God. (Genesis 3) To reverse this act the Lord set in motion a strategy. It involved calling a man, forming a nation, giving a country and sending the Messiah. Only then would the true meaning of happiness be regained. It would cost the Lord much.

It began when God called Abram to begin the plan in Genesis 12:2–3: 'I will make of you a great nation, and I will bless you; I will make your name great, so that you will be a blessing. I will bless those who bless you, and the one who curses you I will curse; and in you all the families of the earth shall be blessed.' This promise must have been overwhelming in the light of Abram's situation.

The story of Abram, later named Abraham by God, is fascinating and challenging. He was a man who trusted God's promises. Over time there were slip–ups and doubts but somehow, he clung to God's unfailing faithfulness. Abraham is God's example for us today. We haven't seen the promised heaven but we believe the One who promised it. In John 14:1–3 Jesus told His disciples He was returning to glory to prepare a place for them. That happened after the cross and resurrection. Since then, followers of Jesus have been pilgrims of faith. As they journey they become discoverers of God's grace and explorers of His Word. There will be many mountain–and–valley experiences on the way. However, God has erected signposts from Abraham's journey to give us directions.

There is the signpost of separation. Abraham, on hearing God's call, was told to get out of Ur of the Chaldeans. This was an idolatrous place. He was to trust God to lead him to the land of promise. We may not be asked to leave our physical surroundings yet when the Lord calls us to Himself there is to be a separation. This will be in the spiritual and behavioural realms. 2 Corinthians 6:16–17: 'As God has said, I will live in them and walk among them, and I will be their God, and they shall be My people. Therefore come out from them, and be separate from them, says the Lord.'

There is the signpost of Trust. Faith for the journey develops as we take one step after the other. At first faith is fed by an encounter with God whereby we know He has saved us. There is an emotional euphoria and a bouncing type of happiness in the heart. Over time this faith commitment will be tested by opposition and circumstances. Then we realise our happiness is not an emotional feeling it is a relationship. It is in knowing Him we grow to trust Him. To be blessed is to be conformed to the will and purposes of our Saviour. (Romans 12:1–3)

There is the signpost to refreshment. Weariness is everyone's experience. Failures, fears and folly nip at our happiness. It's a slow, calculated devouring. Abraham knew all these. To overcome such ruthless bites Abraham either built an altar or returned to one. There he worshipped and sacrificed in the presence of the Lord God. Here he became a most important signpost for us. We need to have our own altars. Places in the heart or special spots where we meet with the Lord. At these altars we deal with any faith–devouring problems. It's from our time with God and His word that we have our 'bites' treated. We also gain instruction on how to be 'bite resistant'. From our special altar we rise up, refreshed, to continue our faith journey.

Today's signpost: 'So if you have been raised with Christ, seek the things that are above, where Christ is seated at the right hand of God. Set your minds on things that are above, not on things that are on earth.' (Colossians 3:1–2)

The Positives and Negatives for Happiness
Day: 14

Key verse: 'Turn my eyes from looking at vanities; give me life in your ways.' (Psalm 119:37)

Positive and negative factors generate a state of happiness within your soul. Negative forces in your Christian life are for your safety. The positive powers are to deepen your appreciation of godly happiness. Psalm 1 covers both these matters. The opening verse talks about heeding the negative to gain happiness.

'Happy are those who do not follow the advice of the wicked or take the path that sinners tread or sit in the seat of scoffers.'

Did you pick up on the descent into unhappiness? The term 'wicked' refers to lawless people. They are described as a restless, turbulent sea casting up mire and dirt (Isaiah 57:20). They have no peace. They have no joy. Their delight is to destroy others by diverting them up a dead–end track. 'Do not be deceived; bad company ruins good morals.' (1 Corinthians 15:33) They also rob their victim of happiness, holiness and heaven. To recognise the negatives of happiness is to take correct protective measures.

'Happy are those who … delight … in the law of the Lord, and on His law they meditate day and night.'

David doesn't define happiness. He reveals its source. David then goes on and speaks about the resulting fruitfulness. As you read through the psalms you will find the writers do define the fruits of godly happiness. Circumstances vary. God does not!

Here we see the set of the heart. The idea of delight is not referring to some glorious sunset or emotional encounter. Rather it points to an act of the individual's will. Apply this verse to yourself. Does your inner being beat with a real joy in reading, understanding and applying God's Word? When a believer would rather read anything else than God's Word a sadness of spirit emerges. A mist casts its presence over the witness and faith of the disciple. Protection against the spiritual mists is in Psalm 37:30–31: 'The mouths of the righteous utter wisdom, and their tongues speak justice. The law of their God is in their hearts; their steps do not slip.'

Biblical meditation does not mean emptying your mind. It doesn't mean hypnotic recitations. Biblical meditation is just what it says. You fix your heart and mind of God's Word choosing some passage to reflect upon. Then you mentally chew it over. Psalm 19:14: 'Let the words of my mouth and the meditation of my heart be acceptable to You, O Lord, my rock and my redeemer.' Happy is the person who does such things. Why?

'They are like trees planted by streams of water, which yield their fruit in its season, and their leaves does not wither.'

This tree isn't a wild bush out in the wilderness with a spring of underground water nearby. It is planted. Happiness isn't an accident! Happiness isn't self–sustaining. Happiness requires planning. It demands irrigation. It needs cultivation. The word for 'streams' does not point to a natural creek or river. It refers to a channel dug for the purpose of watering the tree. When you heed the negative and delight in the positive you are digging a channel for the water of life to flow into your spirit. When you meditate and worship you do a dredging job on that channel. The outcome is a happiness not dominated by outside pressures. It is sustained by the living water of Heaven. Jeremiah was not known for an easy life, but he wrote: 'Blessed are those who trust in the Lord. They shall be like a tree planted by water sending out its roots by the stream. It shall not fear when heat comes, and its leaves shall stay green; in the year of drought it is not anxious, and it does not cease to bear fruit.' (Jeremiah 17:7–8)

Today's signpost: 'This book of the Law shall not depart out of your mouth; you shall meditate on it day and night, so that you may be careful to act in accordance with all that is written in it.' (Joshua 1:8)

Happy are the Poor—Really
Day: 15

Key verse: 'Blessed are you who are poor, for yours is the kingdom of God.' (Luke 6:20)

Upside–down values according to the world. Right–side up for living according to Jesus! This has to be the difference in mindset between the two worldviews. Even for Christians the idea that it is a blessing to be poor is often a bit hard to swallow. How are we to understand this Beatitude? Is it applicable today?

Looking into the accounts of Matthew and Luke, it's apparent they took place on two separate occasions. Matthew's more extensive list is probably explained by being written for a different readership. The issue we have to wrestle with, however, is not only to understand the meaning of 'poor' but also how they can enjoy happiness.

There is no intrinsic righteousness associated with poverty. They share the same sinking rowboat with all other strata of society. Romans 3:22–23 makes this clear: 'There is no distinction, since all have sinned and fall short of the glory of God.' Therefore why are the poor assured of the kingdom of God? This requires a look at the requirements for entering into it.

Jesus said to Nicodemus a person must be born again otherwise he will never see, let alone enter, the kingdom of God. Using another analogy, a person has to be childlike to receive the kingdom. If not, they miss it. In Luke 18:18 the question from a rich ruler about doing something to inherit eternal life throws into sharp contrast the childlikeness demanded. The thief on the cross next to Jesus was as poverty–stricken as a person ever could be. He asked Jesus to remember him when Jesus entered into His kingdom. Jesus took the criminal at his faith statement and said, 'Today you will be with Me in paradise.' (Luke 23:43)

In a confrontation with the chief priests and elders, Jesus again gives insight into how to enter the kingdom. 'Truly I tell you, the tax collectors and the prostitutes are going into the kingdom of God ahead of you. For John came to you in the way of righteousness and you did not believe him, but the tax collectors and the prostitutes believed him; and even after you saw it, you did not change your minds and believe him.' (Matthew 21:31–32)

Can you discern a picture emerging?

Poverty has nothing to do with the wallet! It has everything to do with the heart. A poor man can be as self–willed and proud in self–righteousness as the richest person. The wealthiest man can recognise his moral and spiritual poverty just as surely as the harlot or murderer. The longing for wholeness, forgiveness and happiness must be recognised as outside human attainment or status. Understanding personal need and the inability to earn the reward is meant to make the heart cry out. This is borne out in the Parable of the Pharisee and the Tax Collector (Luke 18:9–14). The Pharisee informed God about his superiority to the lower castes and therefore implied he was not in any need of God's grace. The Tax Collector cried out: 'God, have mercy on me, a sinner.' Jesus used a significant term when He said that this man went home 'justified'. His sense of poverty in the presence of God made him realise his moral and spiritual destitution. It is quite feasible he was financially well–off. His poverty of soul opened the way to an abiding happiness.

Here is the signpost for you and me. The Lord wants us to have an encounter with Him whatever our bank balance. When we meet Him we feel unworthy, unclean and undone. This isn't meant to crush us. Rather, the Lord wants us to cry, 'Lord, have mercy on me, a sinner.' No one who has honestly spoken similar words has been denied his or her plea. Such a cry, however trembling, weak and simple it is, reveals a hunger. Christ will feed the famished soul with heaven's manna. In 1 Corinthians 6:9–10 is a long list of people not welcomed into the kingdom of God. One look at it and you realise it actually includes some of the ones Jesus had accepted. The answer to this is in verse 11: 'This is what some of you use to be. But you were washed, you were sanctified, you were justified in the name of the Lord Jesus Christ and in the Spirit of our God.'

Such are the poor who are blessed when they cry out to the Lord Jesus for His riches.

Today's signpost: 'Listen, my beloved brothers and sisters. Has not God chosen the poor in the world to be rich in faith and to be heirs of the kingdom that He has promised to those who love Him?' (James 2:5)

Purity of Heart Breeds Happiness
Day: 16

Key verse: 'Blessed are the pure in heart, for they will see God.' (Matthew 5:8)

Despair must have swept over the crowd at these words from Jesus. The longing of the heart to see and know God was knocked on the head. How could the human heart be pure, clean, unblemished? Some amongst them must have recalled Job 25:4–6 where Bildad spoke: '… can a mortal be righteous before God? How can one born of a woman be pure? If even the moon is not bright and the stars are not pure in His sight, how much less a mortal, who is a maggot, and a human being, who is a worm?'

This signpost to happiness would have been pointing to a dead end.

I wonder whether or not Jesus was sending out a coded signal about Himself? At His birth certain people had insights that He was the promised One. How could the religious leaders fail to see Jesus as the fulfilment of Scripture? It wasn't from lack of information within the law, the prophets or the writings. Reading the Gospels can only bring us to the conclusion it was impure hearts, sullied by unbelief, self–interest and arrogance. Sounds much like today.

Pure in heart isn't the same as being perfect. The word points to being clean or unblemished. Psalm 24:3–6 asks who was able to stand in the Lord's holy place? The reply — the person who had clean hands and a pure heart, expressions of the outward behaviour and inward disposition. This meant no false dealings or shedding of innocent blood. To approach the presence of God the seeker must have no association with idols and their profanity. The words of his or her mouth must not be camouflage for deceit but instead express truth in unsullied grace. Such an individual will find vindication and happiness before the Lord. Jesus seems to me to have taken these thoughts and inserted deeper meaning. He promised the pure in heart would 'see' God.

Under the old dispensation sin, guilt and defilement were dealt with by the substitutionary sacrifice of an appropriate animal. The offerer took Yahweh at His word and went home justified and pure. In the New Testament dispensation, the fulfilment of those symbolic sacrifices was in Jesus on the cross. Still the question remains about how do we see God? If happiness is seeing God and that depends upon a pure heart, what does 'seeing God' really mean?

Philip asked a similar question recorded in John 14:8—'Lord, show us the Father and we will be satisfied.' Did he grasp the reply? 'Whoever has seen Me has seen the Father.' We do not know how Philip felt. He was probably more perplexed than ever.

Another disciple—this time Thomas the courageous doubter—raised the issue from a different perspective. Not being in attendance at the upper room after the resurrection Thomas was sceptical about the disciples' claims of seeing Jesus. A week later the Lord confronted Thomas. He exclaimed, 'My Lord and my God!' This is an amazing declaration. However Jesus' words to him are even more so. Across the centuries they reach out to us. 'Have you believed because you have seen Me? Blessed are those who have not seen and yet have come to believe.'   Happiness is faith based.

Very few of us will ever receive a vision of Christ Jesus. He has made His meeting ground for us in the preaching of His word and our response. 1 Peter 1:22–23 informs us: 'Now that you have purified your souls by your obedience to the truth ... You have been born anew, not of perishable but of imperishable seed, through the living and enduring Word of God.' To be made pure by the blood of Christ, to be kept pure by its eternal power, means one day we will see God face to face.

Now that is eternal happiness!

Today's signpost: 'For the grace of God has appeared, bringing salvation to all ... while we wait for the blessed hope and the manifestation of the glory of our great God and Saviour, Jesus Christ. He it is who gave Himself for us that He might redeem us from all iniquity and purify for Himself a people of His own who are zealous for good deeds.' (Titus1:11–14)

Weeping has a Use–by Date
Day: 17

Key verse: 'Blessed are you who weep now, for you will laugh.' (Luke 6:21b)

To 'weep' indicates a grief too deep, too real to hide. It breaks out in tears and groans. Weeping is mentioned far more than laughter in Scripture. This is the daily fountain— from untold numbers across uncounted minutes.

Those caught up in the euphoria of following Jesus would have tasted the various flavours of teardrops. Here the Lord spoke not about tears of joy but of sorrow. They were a subjected people despised by the upper classes of their society. The nation was over–taxed and living under the shadow of terrorists. There would also have been many who could echo Psalm 119:136 — 'My eyes shed streams of tears because Your law is not kept'.

Jesus wasn't making some new promise about future happiness. Often the Lord either quoted or alluded to passages from the Jewish Bible. Isaiah 25:6–8 is one of these: 'On this mountain the Lord of hosts will make for all peoples a feast of rich food … He will destroy on this mountain the shroud that is cast over all peoples, the sheet that is spread over all nations; He will swallow up death forever. Then the Lord God will wipe away the tears from all faces; and the disgrace of His people He will take away from all the earth, for the Lord has spoken.'

The Herald of the coming Kingdom encouraged the faithful to hang onto their faith for a better tomorrow. They would face injustices, encounter corruption and suffer oppression. All these things would make their tears flow. Each drop, however, would be a memorial to their faithfulness under pressure. Those who knew Scripture and believed it would understand the confidence of Jesus. Isaiah looked forward to a day promised by the Lord God. Isaiah 65:17–19 recalls God's words: 'I am about to create new heavens and a new earth; the former things shall not be remembered or will come to mind. But be glad and rejoice forever in what I am creating; for I am about to create Jerusalem as a joy, and its people a delight. I will rejoice in Jerusalem and delight in My people; no more shall the sound of weeping be heard in it, or the cry of distress.'

The words of the prophets on this matter have still to be fulfilled. They will be!

What then, do the words of Jesus about mourning and being comforted mean for us? Virtually the same as when He spoke them. We still shed tears more than we laugh. Those tears may flow down our cheeks. They may be unseen falling within our hearts or minds. Weeping may have many causes: where we live, the opposition we face, the trials facing us, or simply a deep sorrow over the plight of others. We may cry because our faith offends. Paul spoke about his tears in Philippians 3:18. He was not crying on his or the church's behalf. Paul wrote how he cried over those who did the persecuting. Why? Because he knew their destiny! Do we shed similar tears? We may also cry in the same manner as Peter. Remember, he denied his Lord. When he realised it Peter wept bitterly. None of us will be immune from such tears. How wonderful to know the grace of forgiveness offered by Jesus. He heals the breach, wipes the tears and comforts the heart.

In the closing book of Scripture, there is this assurance concerning the future. It speaks of the time when the Holy City, the New Jerusalem, comes down out of heaven from God. The beauty of this event is described as a bride coming to meet her husband. Within the Bible there are a few occasions when a loud shout resonates from Heaven. This is one of those occasions. This is the moment when weeping will cease. Revelation 21:2–4 says, 'God Himself will be with them; He will wipe away every tear from their eyes, death will be no more; mourning and crying and pain will be no more.'

The words of Jesus and His apostle are yet to be fulfilled. They will be!

Today's signpost: 'When the Lord turned again the captivity of Zion, we were like them that dream. Then was our mouth filled with laughter, and our tongue with singing.' (Psalm 126:1–2 KJV)

Is it Ears or Eyes for Happiness?
Day: 18

Key verse: 'Jesus said to Thomas, "Have you believed because you have seen me? Blessed are those who have not seen and yet have come to believe."' (John 20:29)

'Show me and I'll believe' is the excuse of people trying to sidestep making a decision regarding faith. If happiness depended upon the simple act of seeing would there be less miserable individuals today? No! When a person bases their judgements merely on what they see they end up disappointed. Eyes can be deceived. The sleight of hands of a magician proves this point. The other implication is that no visually impaired person would ever believe.

God bypassed the eye for the ear! To be blessed by God is to believe what He promised. Remember, the Church's beginning was in an age when few had access to books. The reading of Scripture and other works was an art performed by the qualified. We may think the eye has replaced the ear as the channel for happiness. I doubt it. We may read many words but not hear their message in our heart and mind. We will always need the Holy Spirit to make what we read to be heard in our inner being. We still need to listen.

Why is the ear gate the entrance point for experiencing Godly happiness?

Hebrews 11:6 says, 'Without faith it is impossible to please God, for whoever would approach Him must believe that He exists and that He rewards those who seek Him.' After the day of Pentecost in Acts 2 the apostles and evangelists continually pointed hearers of their message back to the Scriptures. Their authority and challenge is imbedded in the simple yet awesome statement, 'it is written'. (1 Corinthians 15:3–4) This holds true even today!

The words of Peter reveal the enduring power of what is heard and received from the Gospel. In his first letter to a scattered and suffering Church, he stressed the eternal wealth of their faith in the Gospel. As gold was purified from its dross by fire the apostle compared it to their afflictions. Gold ultimately perishes or wears away. Faith under the fire of persecution is refined and increased. How is that possible? Because the ears have fed the heart. The heart then made the eyes to see the Lord's purposes triumphing through the affliction! This gave believers reason to rejoice—not from what they saw or felt but from what they knew. How? Because of what they had heard and believed!

In worship we can often sing with sincerity: 'I want to see You, Lord'. This will not happen until we leave this planet or He comes to collect us. The more biblical expression would be to sing something like: 'Lord, I want to hear Your word speaking to my heart. I want Your Holy Spirit to make it clear to me.' To long to see Him is the natural longing of the heart. However our spiritual happiness will only grow and blossom as we hear His Word and obey it. Perhaps this helps us to understand why the forces of the antichrist oppose biblical teaching. They aim to limit our affection for, interest in and study of Scripture. If they succeed, our sense of happiness will become a fleeting and spasmodic experience.

When you threw yourself upon the mercy of God, a spiritual reaction took place within your being. You became a new person. Within your inner self there are tremendous possibilities for heaven's purposes to possess you. One such feature is that which Jesus promised in our key verse. You will know His abiding happiness, not from seeing, but from having ears to hear His Word and believe.

Today's signpost: 'The Lord God has given me the tongue of a teacher that I may know the Word, that I may know how to sustain the weary with a word. Morning by morning He wakens my ear to listen as those who are taught. The Lord God has opened my ear, and I was not rebellious, I did not turn backwards.' (Isaiah 50:4–5)

The Place in which Happiness Abides
Day: 19

Key verse: 'Serve the Lord with fear, with trembling kiss His feet, or He will be angry, and you are will perish in the way; for His wrath is quickly kindled. Happy are all who take refuge in Him.' (Psalm 2:12)

Safe houses exist for those who are in need of protection. The only requirements are the person recognises his or her need and goes to the appropriate place. In Numbers 35 we find six locations nominated as cities of refuge. These towns were set aside as sanctuaries for people in danger of retribution as the result of the death of another person. As there was no police force as we understand it today, the next–of–kin to the victim was honour–bound to track down the slayer and extract justice. The pursuer was called the Avenger of Blood. Cities of Refuge provided safety from this person. It also provided time for the appointed leaders to assess the case and pass judgement.

As with other similar history recorded in the Old Testament, these cities of refuge have a spiritual application. Some of us may wonder why we need a place of safety. If there is a need, then from whom are we actually fleeing? This drives us to the biblical understanding of God. Currently, He is promoted as the God of Love. True! However, He is also the holy God. John 3:36 makes this clear: 'Whoever believes in the Son has eternal life; but whoever disobeys the Son will not see life, but must endure God's wrath.' That takes us back to our verse for today. Our heart and mind should tremble at the holiness of God, knowing our sinful nature.

The Gospel informs us that we are part of a sinful and rebellious world. As such, we have contributed to the death of Jesus. That means God the Father must become the Avenger of Blood to us. At the same time the wrath of God is aroused when people call Him a liar and despise His offer of salvation in Christ. Do we really imagine the Lord doesn't feel anger when His creation and moral code are violated?

How can we find a safe place from His anger and justice? In God's mercy He provided the place. When Jesus called out, 'Father, forgive them for they know not what they do,' He turned our rebellion into ignorance. At the same moment, Jesus raised a place of refuge from the Father's wrath. It is the most secure and eternal refuge in which to be safe, to be forgiven, to be blessed.

Providing it for us does not automatically mean we are in it. We have to make a personal choice to accept Him as Lord and Saviour. In reaching out to Him, He embraces us and draws us into Himself. The spiritual reality of this is summed up in the simple phrase 'in Him' or 'in Christ'. Happiness is in knowing that we have kissed the Son's feet. This is a picture of our submission, gratitude and faith.

Psalm 91 is magnificent! It is actually Messianic. His experience and triumph has become His place of refuge for believers. We, therefore, can find a deep sense of comfort knowing we abide in Him. 'You who live in the shelter of the Most High, who abide in the shadow of the Almighty, will say to the Lord, "My refuge and my fortress; my God, in whom I trust."'

The nursery rhyme *The Three Little Pigs* often makes me think about people's attitude towards salvation. One pig built his house of straw. It is easy—and the material is plentiful. The house was easily destroyed. It's the same for those who put their hope in their goodness. The second pig built with sticks. Slightly more up–market, but easily burnt! A picture of those trusting in religious observance! The third pig built with bricks. These would have been prepared and supplied by another. It was a more substantial building and secure from the breath of the wolf. This third pig is for me a picture of those who have built their salvation in the Rock called Jesus Christ.

Happiness is in knowing you dwell in a secure place from the wrath of God. Peace comes from the certainty that you are secure from condemnation. Being 'in Christ' offers the greatest security possible.

Today's signpost: 'God is our refuge and strength, a very present help in trouble.' (Psalm 46:1)

The Blessing of Reproof
Day: 20

Key verse: 'How happy is the one whom God reproves; therefore do not despise the discipline of the Almighty.' (Job 5:17)

The world class golfer was having a difficult time. His swing wasn't smooth, the drive from the tee didn't fly true and the fairway seemed a stranger to the ball. This had been a developing problem over the past few tournaments and wasn't getting better. His enjoyment in the game was seriously eroded—not to mention his success! Frustration and self–doubt ruled. He knew it was time to see his coach. Correcting whatever had intruded into his game was essential for success and happiness.

There are times in our Christian life when we know things are not quite right. We are on the course but we are not 'swinging correctly'. We need a coach to look at our game. Who will evaluate those factors that make us miss the fairway and end up in the rough? Hear the invitation from God: 'Come now, let us argue it out …' (Isaiah 1:18a). The word 'argue' is the same as 'reprove', used by Job's friend.

God wants to keep us on the fairway. He wants us to avoid the traps that surround the green. How does He do this? In John 16:7 Jesus announced to His team that He was going to leave them. However, they would not have to play the 'game' in their own strength. This was important as they would face devious opposition intent upon making them lose the game or be miserable in it. Who was to be the coach for those on Christ's team? The Counsellor! He is called the Holy Spirit.

Like the golfer, we may need to return to the basics. Do we need to place ourselves once again under His teaching? He invites us to talk over our frustrations, failures and disappointments. Then we need to go to the practice tee and recalibrate our 'swing'. Regaining the rhythm and timing won't come immediately, but it will happen! When that glimmer of being on the right track begins, a renewed sense of enjoyment warms the soul.

No Christian can be happy sitting out the game. Neither can we be content with always being in the bunker. Happiness means you're in the game, hitting the ball on the fairways and playing by the rules. Once again, the 'game' is worth playing.

Why does the Almighty bother coaching us? Because He wants us to know happiness even up against antagonistic and unfair opposition! The Lord doesn't want us to quit the game when facing such difficulties. He will draw us aside and begin teaching us how to master the game. He will also help us in our dealings with those who want us to fail. His methods are custom-made and they vary greatly. The purpose of discipline is to develop in us wisdom, self–discipline and understanding! These factors are so important when it's our turn to play. We need to know what 'club' to use, the dangers faced, the 'distance' to overcome, the prevailing conditions and support or otherwise of the onlookers.

There are times when we aren't keen on the self–discipline required by the Coach. He has great patience, but do we sometimes stretch it a bit? Maybe we need to recognise our reluctance, confess it and quote Jeremiah 10:24: 'Correct me, O Lord, but in just measure; not in Your anger or You will bring me to nothing.' Accept the fact discipline doesn't make us bubble over with delight. However, after we discover the benefits, we develop a more positive disposition. Frustration sinks. Happiness rises.

Today's signpost: 'Happy are those whom you discipline, O Lord, and whom you teach out of your law.' (Psalm 94:12)

Enjoying the Second Mile
Day: 21

Key verse: 'If anyone forces you to go one mile, go also the second mile.' (Matthew 5:41)

The law of Roman occupation included a compulsion to carry a soldier's baggage. It could not be more than one mile, but there was no escaping the touch of the sword. It pressed a person into service. Imagine the resentment of the carrier. Taken from what he was doing, he would have no time to make other arrangements, no opportunity to explain to family or employer. One mile forward and the same mile back. The sense of injustice and bitterness would grow with each step. A victim mentality would be born, perhaps never to die.

The challenge by Jesus must have felt like salt sprinkled on lash wounds. What was Jesus saying to His disciples, then and now? Don't be a victim. Be the master over the situation. The Roman soldier wouldn't be open to talking with an inferior subject and would simply expect a sullen carrier. How things would change when a follower of Christ would volunteer to go that extra mile. What an opportunity to explain why he did it. Here was a chance to talk about Jesus. Using such unwanted intrusions to witness on behalf of the Lord prevents us from feeling powerless.

Happiness in such uncertain circumstances deepens by doing the unexpected. The New Testament reveals how the Holy Spirit shows the oppressed and powerless ways to maintain their dignity. Matthew 5:44–45: 'Love your enemies and pray for those who persecute you, so that you may be children of your Father in Heaven.' Far from being insipid or a shield for the weak, the principle is unconquerable.

If we are honest, our initial reaction to an imposition is usually an upsurge from our carnal nature. Most of us don't like being made to do things against our interests or comfort. Then the indwelling presence of Christ surges to the front. He makes us aware of His mind on the matter. We are faced with the choice. Do what we have to do with a bad attitude, and thereby be a victim. Do it as unto Him, enjoy His pleasure and be an overcomer.

There is a Biblical illustration of the Roman law in operation. It's recorded in Matthew 27:32: 'As they went out, they came upon a man from Cyrene named Simon; they compelled this man to carry His (Christ's) cross.' How unpleasant that would have been! How humiliating as he struggled under its weight in the sight of a crowd caught up in the frenzy of the moment! Three days later, what would have been his feelings? In Mark's account we learn this man was the father of Alexander and Rufus. So? In Romans 16:13 Rufus and his mother are lovingly mentioned in greetings by Paul. From being a 'passer–by' compelled to carry the stake for Christ's crucifixion, Simon and family became loyal disciples of Jesus.

One of the biggest problems associated with going the first mile and only the first mile in a bad attitude is what it breeds. It is like deadly spiritual bacteria infecting our sense of joy. It also stunts spiritual growth. Such a condition is produced by injured pride and impotence. It multiplies alarmingly.

Today we do not live under Roman law. However, there are people inside and outside the Church who still have this dominating power over us. This may even be the sad fact of life within a marriage or in a parent–child relationship. The best antidote for spiritual bacteria is to take Christ's antidote. Go the second mile. The imposer may not change. You will!

The apostle Peter writes about believers living under such stressful and unpleasant situations. He doesn't make light of their suffering but, using the example of Jesus. Peter points the way to safe–guarding one's health and joy in Christ. 1 Peter 3:9: 'Do not repay evil for evil or abuse for abuse; but, on the contrary, repay with a blessing. It is for this that you were called—that you might inherit a blessing.'

Today's signpost: 'Do all things without murmuring and arguing, so that you may be blameless and innocent, children of God without blemish in the midst of a crooked and perverse generation, in which you shine like stars in the world.' (Philippians 2:14–15)

Christ's Enlistment Slogan
Day: 22

Key verse: 'If the world hates you, be aware that it hated Me before it hated you.' (John 15:18)

Jesus could never do work in an advertising agency. Can you imagine him as the enlisting officer for a PR firm? Why? Simply because He tells it as it is—no deceit, no false promises, no soft peddling of the difficulties!

Before the crucifixion Jesus had a few hours alone with His disciples. They weren't too sure about what was going to happen but knew it would not be pleasant. Then Jesus gives them a motivational message. It was and remains unique. 'I have chosen you out of the world—therefore the world hates you. Remember the word I said to you, "Servants are not greater than their master". If they persecuted Me, they will persecute you …They will do all these things to you on account of My name…' (John 15:19–21)

Why then, did they sign up? On the other side of the cross, I'm of the opinion they had second thoughts. In fact, each one in some way betrayed their Master. The resolve of the disciples was in its death throes in the Garden of Gethsemane. What brought it back to life? What made being hated for Christ Jesus a badge of honour and not a cause for embarrassment? The cross and resurrection!

Many leaders in Christendom have substituted Christ's enlistment slogan with something else. They prefer a more genteel, more pleasing statement. It could be: 'Trust Jesus and He will make you a person of influence.' Another could be: 'Jesus offers you a prosperous future' or 'Salvation is God's health care plan for your life.' No wonder there is a huge drop–out rate when things get rough.

Discipleship has a cost. It needs some spelling out. Jesus' idea of happiness is an alternative concept to the commonly held view. For instance, take: 'Blessed are you when people hate you, and when they exclude you and revile you, and defame you on account of the Son of Man.' (Luke 6:22) Immediately Jesus follows that with: 'Rejoice!' Why? Because you are on the right side of God's promises, purpose and kingdom!

Jesus didn't say that being treated in such a manner was fun. Nor did He encourage His followers to behave in an obnoxious way to arouse animosity. Jesus set the standard. Peter's description of Jesus' earthly ministry is revealing. 'God anointed Jesus of Nazareth with the Holy Spirit and with power; how He went about doing good and healing all who were oppressed by the devil, for God was with Him.' (Acts 10:38) This was despite the opposition, slander and malice of the authorities.

What enables Christ's followers to remain true under defamation, defilement, denigration and death? What keeps the sense of blessing beating within? It is more than making a decision to accept His salvation. It is more than knowing forgiveness and cleansing. Perseverance and joy come from knowing and enjoying Jesus Christ, regardless!

Paul called Christ's disciples 'clay jars' who hold a glorious treasure. It is the fragrance of Christ, the Gospel of grace and being recipients of Christ's indwelling presence. (2 Corinthians 2–4) To realise this will underscore our fragility and Christ's ability. He is our strength. Therefore, all our experiences are meant to express what is within. Paul wrote to the Philippians: 'I want to know Christ and the power of His resurrection.' As the ungodly rise up against the Church we can declare: You hate us, Christ loves us. You crush us, Christ keeps us. You oppose us, Christ strengthens us. You don't know Him, Christ has made Himself known to us.

The cross speaks of Christ Jesus' love and the world's hate. When we picked up our cross to follow Jesus we opened ourselves to know both features. His happiness has become ours!

Today's signpost: 'Consider my affliction and my trouble, and forgive all my sins. Consider how many are my foes, and with what violent hatred they hate me. O guard my life, and deliver me; do not let me be put to shame, for I take refuge in You. May integrity and uprightness preserve me, for I wait for You.' (Psalm 25:18–21)

The Marriage Celebration
Day: 23

Key verse: 'Then the angel said to me, "Write this: Blessed those who are invited to the wedding supper of the Lamb."' (Revelation 19:9)

God arranged the first marriage in the Garden of Eden. The final marriage will be arranged by God in the heavens. The first one became a tragedy. The final one is an eternal triumph. Our earthly marriages get their significance and beauty from the Judeo– Christian faith's teaching. Without this, the marriage symbolism and its culmination is robbed of its meaning, mystery and majesty.

Why did the angel call the Bridegroom 'the Lamb' instead of Jesus Christ? Possibly to reinforce the amazing and wonderful relationship He has with His wife. This is nowhere better expressed than in Ephesians 5:25–30. Within those verses you discover the Lord chose the most unlikely 'girl' to be His bride. Jesus had to rescue her from the slavery of sin, break the chains of degradation and corruption, wash her and clothe her. Her offences against heaven meant she bore the death penalty. Jesus took her place and paid her sentence. His righteousness overcame her iniquity and death's grip. This was verified by His resurrection. He then breathed into her His resurrection life. This caused her to be radiant, blameless and without blemish. Now she was ready to reign with Him eternally.

Whether we are single or married, separated or divorced, the Lord wants us all to be part of His wedding supper. He wants to share His happiness with us. The question then arises 'how do we know we have been invited?'

'The Spirit and the bride say, "Come". And let everyone who hears say, "Come". And let everyone who is thirsty come. Let anyone who wishes take the water of life as a gift.' (Revelation 22:17) It is an open invitation, yet only those who are thirsty will respond. What do they want to drink? The water of grace! It will cleanse their sin–scorched and morally parched lives with forgiveness. It will refresh their weary and heavy–laden hearts.

It will give them a new beginning. Now they can blossom in righteousness and truth as well as know the joy of peace with God. Where can they find such a thirst–quenching flow? Jesus revealed it to the woman at the well in John 4! He is the fountain. This life–giving water is available simply by requesting that He give it to us.

A wedding custom at that time in Israel was to give each guest a special wedding garment. It was an indication of their acceptance of the invitation, as well as a gift from the groom. This also applies to us. We can only be present at the heavenly wedding clothed in the righteousness given by our Lord Jesus. Isaiah 61:10 says, 'I will greatly rejoice in the Lord; my whole being shall exult in my God for He has clothed me with garments of salvation, He has covered me with the robe of righteousness …'

Another dimension to our happiness is summed up in Jesus' promise to the original disciples. He told them He was going back to His Father's house to prepare many rooms. This was the bridegroom's responsibility as he prepared to receive his bride and take her home. When the Lord told them this He promised to return to take them back with Him to the place He had prepared. This is further emphasised in the prayer in John 17. In it He said He wanted His people to be where He would be and to see His glory. The key verse for today looks forward to the day when the promise will be realised. In between the promise and its fulfilment, the bride–in–waiting is to trust her Bridegroom's word. She will face many challenges, endure much opposition and experience many temptations to be unfaithful. What keeps her faithful, true and pure? Knowing her Lord keeps His word because of the price He paid to make her His own.

Today's signpost: 'Therefore, brothers and sisters, be all the more eager to confirm your call and election … For in this way, entry into the eternal kingdom of our Lord and Saviour Jesus Christ will be richly provided for you.' (2 Peter 1:10–11)

Cause and Effect
Day: 24

Key verse: 'If you know these things, you are blessed if you do them.' (John 13:17)

Little Things Mean a Lot was a popular song some years ago and sung by many artists. I'd like to rephrase that line in relation to the Lord's guidelines for happiness. 'Little words imply a lot' would sum up our key verse for today. Notice the promise to the disciples in the upper room. It's dependent, not on Him, but on a little word motivating them. It is the word 'do'.

Happiness isn't a theory. Nor is it a spiritual emotion. The secret from the upper room is this: godly happiness is the result of moral, relational and spiritual motion. The Lord stressed this on many occasions and linked it with a person's love for Him. 'They who have My commands and keep them are those who love Me.' (John 14:21a) Much later, the apostle John would add in a letter that the Lord's commands are not burdensome. (1 John 5:3)

I'm sure you will agree that there are times when what the Lord requires of us seems a bit much. We want to debate it. We want to seek alternatives when it takes us out of our comfort zone. We question His intentions when we cannot see the 'why'!

Ultimately, it comes down to the Lord speaking to us in words similar to those from the upper room: 'You do not know now what I am doing, but later you will understand.' (John 13:7)

Perhaps the best illustration occurs in John 2 where it describes Jesus' first miracle in Cana. When the wine ran out at the wedding Jesus was put on the spot by His mother. She instructed the servants to do whatever Jesus requested. Imagine their perplexity when He told them to fill the large jars with water. Did they feel their jobs were on the line and their integrity would be damaged forever? Did they worry that Jesus would be laughed at? Did they tremble as the governor of the feast took the first sip? Their relief must have been huge when the chief steward praised the wine.

What does this incident teach us? Even though you don't understand Christ's command, just do it! The 'why' will become apparent after, and not before, obedience!

There are untold numbers of unhappy disciples inside and outside the Church. The reason in most cases will be traced back to a failure to do the 'do'. James 4:17 corroborates this: 'Anyone, then, who knows the right thing to do and fails to do it, commits sin.'

The word describing 'sin' means falling short. To fall short of the Lord's standard means we rob ourselves of the happiness He desired for us. This sense of loss makes us react in a negative manner towards God. We imagine He is picking on us. Our spiritual negativity produces 'bad breath'. In turn, it permeates our personalities and makes us unpleasant company. What is the answer to such bad breath? Not prayer! Not promises! Not philanthropy! Simply 'do' what has been commanded.

Again we ask 'why?'

The significance of the 'doing' is dramatically illustrated in Matthew 25:31–46 in the parable of the sheep and goats. The inner reality of an individual nation's relationship to the Lord was expressed in how they treated Christ's people. The nations with the 'sheep' nature cared for and protected the people in need. The nations with the 'goat' nature didn't lift a finger to help.

The link between the nations and Christ's disciples is apparent. What mattered wasn't talking or theologising about everyone's merits. It was the doing or not doing which revealed their unseen relationship with the Lord. Matthew 25:40 says, 'Truly I tell you, just as you did it to one of the least of these members of My family, you did it to Me.'

Happiness is not an emotion which can flourish amidst apathy, indifference and neglect. The Lord's happiness within is the result of faith activating the will to 'do'.

Today's signpost: 'Teach me to do Your will, for you are my God. Let Your good spirit lead me on level ground.' (Psalm 143:10)

Happiness' Enrichment Centre
Day: 25

Key verse: 'Happy are those who live in Your house, ever singing Your praise.' (Psalm 84:4)

A warrior with the gift of writing and a fine singing voice wrote this psalm. Being a descendent of Levi, he was from the clan assigned to guard the Tabernacle. Also he was a member of the choristers. David had organised them to sing the praises of Yahweh within the Tabernacle worship. (1 Chronicles 25)

For him this was an unending source of privilege and pleasure. As you read the psalm it is evident a yearning developed when he was absent from the Tabernacle. 'My soul longs, indeed it faints, for the courts of the Lord; my heart and my flesh sing for joy to the living God.' (Psalm 84:2) As one of the Sons of Korah, he had special ministries. It's clear he didn't take it for granted.

The Christian faith has no defined place such as the Tabernacle or Temple in the same way as the psalmist had, yet we do belong to God's household. Paul's word to Timothy makes this claim very clear. 'You may know how one ought to behave in the household of God, which is the church of the living God, the pillar and bulwark of the truth.' (1 Timothy 3:15) Within that 'household' surely a sense of wonder and gratitude will give us a desire for worship. 'Let the Word of Christ dwell in you richly; teach and admonish one another with all wisdom, and with gratitude in your hearts sing psalms, hymns and spiritual songs from the Spirit to God.' (Colossians 3:16)

Looking back on a past pilgrimage the psalmist recounts: 'Happy are those whose strength in You, in whose heart are the highways to Zion. As they go through the Valley of Baca they make it a place of springs …' (Psalm 84:5–6)

A sense of mission wrapped in hope moved the pilgrims' feet. They knew they walked through difficult, dangerous and dry places. The pilgrims faced these issues with a determination to overcome the obstacles in their pathway. Each one had an inner compulsion. They were on their way to worship the Lord in His holy Temple.

Spiritual happiness overcame physical tiredness. They had a destination and a purpose.

As Christians, we are on a pilgrimage to glory. We will travel through many unpleasant experiences along the way. What will keep us on the move to our heavenly destination? The joy of the Lord!

If we take our eyes off the Lord, our sense of wonder will be lost. Then our difficult environment will never be transformed into a place of springs. We will miss the refreshing waters that, together with God, we could have carved out of the situation. Those looking to you or me for inspiration on the journey would be disappointed at this loss.

Notice: it is a passage through, not a full stop! This should remind us of Psalm 23:4. 'Even though *I walk through* the darkest valley, I fear no evil; for You are with me, Your rod and Your staff—they comfort me.' (emphasis added).

Throughout Scripture the desire of God has been to dwell with and travel alongside His people. While on that journey He would experience their hardships. He would overrule the discomfort and difficulties of their experiences so as to ensure their happiness and His glory. Jesus followed this up when He told them to go and make disciples of all nations, promising to travel with them until the end of the age. (Matthew 28:19–20)

The happiness we should enjoy on our pilgrimage with the Household of Faith can be damaged. It happens when we fail to nourish our understanding of the Lord Jesus and to refresh our worship of Him. The apostle Peter was well aware of this. In his second letter he gave some worthwhile tips for travellers. To prevent spiritual rot, apathy and disintegration, certain spiritual disciplines need to be added. (2 Peter 1:3–11)

This member of the Sons of Korah sums up our daily signpost. May it ring true in your life and mine.

Today's signpost: 'O Lord of Hosts, happy is everyone who trusts in You.' (Psalm 84:12)

Foundation for Happiness
Day: 26

Key verse: 'Happy are those whose transgression is forgiven, whose sin is covered. Happy are those to whom the Lord imputes no iniquity, and in whose spirit there is no deceit.' (Psalm 32:1–2)

How is the promise of forgiveness possible?

Forgiveness in these two verses covers our corrupt and rebellious thought life, our deliberate acts of breaking God's commands and our soul's perverseness. We tend to treat these matters lightly. The lighter we view them the less we value forgiveness. This results in a poor appreciation of the wonder of our Lord's substitutionary death and His gift of happiness.

Transgression means crossing the boundary into forbidden territory. Adam crossed the line when he shared in the fruit of the forbidden tree in Genesis 3. Ever since, his descendents have been jumping over God's moral and spiritual boundaries. We have no excuses, since those 'keep out' signs have been impressed into our conscience (Romans 2:14–15).

Can the Lord God, whose very nature is holy, simply wave His royal sceptre and say, 'You're forgiven'? This idea would conflict with His justice and righteousness. God can only proclaim forgiveness because the offences against Him have been paid.

What are some of those issues in God's eyes which had to be dealt with before He could offer forgiveness to anyone?

The Father's wrath had to be satisfied.

This was beyond the scope of any human due to their infection with the very thing which angered God. This is why it was necessary for Jesus Christ to come into this world. 'In this is love, not that we loved God, but that he loved us and sent his Son to be the atoning sacrifice for our sins'. (1

John 4:10) The word 'atoning' presents the idea of satisfying the righteous and judicious anger of the Father against humankind's rebellion. In the old covenant, atonement meant 'to cover' the offences through sacrifice of an innocent and unblemished animal. Christ is, at the same time, the One who satisfied the Father's righteous anger and covers and cleanses our sinfulness. Many find it hard to imagine God expressing wrath. This is because they don't see the total revelation He has given of Himself.

The wages of sin had to be cashed in.

Romans 6:23a says this means death! Here is our personal problem. If we paid for our own sins how could we ever rise from the dead! Life would be robbed of peace and happiness, let alone any hope of Heaven. The wonder of wonders is that Jesus Christ stood in our individual place of judgement. He died our death. (1 Peter 3:24) Because of His righteousness and being without sin, Jesus was able to rise again. Jesus is the reason why we can stand before the Father and not be condemned. (Read Romans 8. See also *Captured by Calvary* for further insight). His victory becomes ours by a deliberate act of faith seizing God's grace. This is nectar to the longing heart seeking forgiveness.

Silencing the accusations of the powers of darkness!

For many a believer the skeletons of the past can be continually thrown up in their minds. These ghosts steal our abiding happiness. What is our defence? The cross of Christ and His poured–out life! According to Colossians 2:13–15 we have received forgiveness, been made alive and all the charges against us have been cancelled. We are no longer in debt or condemned. The powers and authorities have been trampled under the cross!

Here is the sheer miracle of Christ and the cross. God has made it possible for us to be washed free from all sin and transgression. He declared us pardoned. By that decree our heavenly Father ceases to remember our offences. We cannot be blackmailed by the powers of darkness. We cannot forget, however, our memories have written over them: 'Pardoned'!

There is much more to be discovered about the wonder of forgiveness. Read Scripture and let your spirit drink deeply of the gift of grace which is foundational for temporal and eternal happiness.

Today's signpost: 'But there is forgiveness with You, so that You may be revered.' (Psalm 130:4)

Protected by the Conscience
Day: 27

Key verse: 'Blessed are those who have no reason to condemn themselves because of what they approve.' (Romans 14:22)

Meat or vegetables was the question. What was the answer? Here was a vital issue the Christians from paganism had to face. In our secular western society such a problem appears ludicrous. However it wasn't a laughing matter in the apostles' time.

Why was it such an issue? Every area of life in the ancient world was dominated by religion and its observances. In particular, the meat at the local butcher's probably had been sacrificed to one of the city's many gods. Some converts to Christ Jesus couldn't handle eating such meat. For others it wasn't a big deal.

What caused the strife? A person's conscience! It isn't easy to live as a Christian in a secular or idolatrous world. As we come out of an anti–christian culture or an indifferent society strange 'barnacles' cling to our minds. These barnacles cause lots of adjustment problems. God's Word tries to scrape them from our inner being.

1 Corinthians 10:23–33 offers good advice for personal happiness on non–essential matters. Live in God's sight what are His requirements for you according to His Word. This will become God's spiritual fitness program individually designed. Therein is the challenge for each disciple. They must know the difference between two areas. One, the unchanging fundamentals of the faith and two, God's permissive will on non–essential matters. The mature believer must allow God to lead a new believer into spiritual maturity.

The Holy Spirit captured and converted you through the Gospel message. He changed your spiritual location from darkness to light. However, He didn't pump into you all the wisdom and power of the ages. A believer has to assimilate knowledge and growth. Knowledge of the Christian lifestyle will reset the conscience as well as the mind. Growth will take place as the believer lives out the knowledge.

How wonderful it is to experience the transforming power of God. Our consciences prior to conversion sought in vain to impress God. This was by personal deeds, promises and ritual. Hebrews 6:1 and 9:14 defines them as 'dead works'. One of the first steps in gaining a healthy and vibrant conscience is repentance. Then we hand over such dead works to the Lord for removal.

Hebrews 10:22 says, 'Let us approach (God) with a true heart ... with our hearts sprinkled clean from an evil conscience ...' Personal happiness blossoms when the conscience has been cleansed. The defilements of lies, self–righteousness and unbelief are removed! This inner liberty also delivers us from being the judge and jury of other people's habits.

Paul's conscience must have had a major makeover after his Damascus road experience. He thought his defence of the Mosaic Law, the imprisoning and murder of Christians and defaming Jesus was righteous. Confronted by the risen Christ, he realised the need of a whole new life. I wonder what inner struggles he had in those hidden years before bursting upon the missionary scene. The degree will differ but our readjustments would have been no less intense. What a wonderful sense of joy floods the spirit when our conscience is at peace. The Holy Spirit applies God's grace and word to cleanse and remove dead works.

As we grow in faith and understanding, so too will the depth and quality of our happiness. There will be times when the calmness of the conscience will be aroused. It will be quieted as we handle our sensitive conscience biblically.

Today's Signpost: 'Indeed, this is our boast, the testimony of our conscience: we have behaved in the world with frankness and godly sincerity, not by earthly wisdom but with the grace of God.' (2 Corinthians 1:12)

Where Fear and Happiness Embrace
Day: 28

Key verse: 'Happy is the one who is never without fear.' (Proverbs 28:14a)

Mentioning fear and happiness in the same breath seems like an oxymoron. That is a figure of speech using words of opposite meanings or suggestions such as a 'wise fool'. Can you be happy in a relationship of fear?

We are reminded that the fear of God is wisdom. There is also the warning about meeting God, who is a consuming fire. (Hebrews 12:29) That doesn't generate many positive vibes for happiness. We know we are combustible!

However, when we accept Jesus as our Lord we can call God our heavenly Father. Should we fear or tremble in the presence of the one we call 'Father'? 1 John 4:18 tells us: 'There is no fear in love, but perfect loves casts out fear; for fear has to do with punishment and whoever fears has not reached perfection in love.'

Our personal sense of happiness with the Lord God Almighty rests upon His perfect love. What is our tangible expression from history and Scripture that confirms such love? The cross!

There isn't any way possible for us to possess and express perfect love. Our natural and justified fear of God must be dealt with by God alone. We cannot bribe Him to remove our fear by our promises and good deeds. What happens when we know we have hurt our heavenly Father's heart? Fear either creeps in or surges like a tsunami over our soul. The thought of being called into His presence in such a state doesn't produce happiness.

We also understand there is only one place to 'hide'. It is the same place where our happiness can be restored. We are urged not to sin. The Lord God knew we would fail in–spite of our best endeavours to live up to His calling consistently! Therefore, He provided an advocate: 'Jesus Christ the righteous; and He is the atoning sacrifice for our sins.' (1 John 2:2) Recognition of our attitude or behaviour should move us to repentance.

This in turn impels us to beseech our advocate to plead our case before our heavenly Father.

Unfortunately, something within us rises up with doubt. Can we really be sure of forgiveness? Will those erected barriers be removed? 1 John 3:20 tells us: 'Whenever our hearts condemn us … God is greater than our hearts, and He knows everything.' In other words it isn't how we feel but what we believe. Our trust rests on the promise and authority of Christ Jesus.

Happiness in the presence of our God actually grows out of fear. We develop an aversion to bringing dishonour on His name. The Scriptures we read and study nourish our spiritual life. Above that, the desire to know and exalt Him reigns. Therefore, our understanding of fear is altered. No longer is it dread. Now it is love enriched by awe. No one who really loves will consciously hurt the one they love. Call it fear if you like; I'd call it devotion.

Happiness isn't a one–off experience. Our happiness must be fed with the approved diet of heaven. In His recipe book for healthy, godly living, foods fit for our spirits are to be found. They are already prepared by heaven's Master Chef, the Holy Spirit. His pantry never lacks what you need from day to day. His invitation is for you to come and dine around His table. Good company and good food is a recipe for abundant happiness.

Today's signpost: 'But this is the one to whom I will look, to the humble and contrite in spirit, who trembles at My word.' (Isaiah 66:2b)

The Refreshment of Happiness
Day: 29

Key verse: 'Live lives that are self–controlled, upright, and godly, while we wait for the blessed hope and the manifestation of the glory of our great God and Saviour, Jesus Christ.' (Titus 2:12–13)

Without hope, a man is inwardly dead. He may move and breathe but life has, in reality, exited his being. Hope is the human spirit's way of lighting fiery beacons in the dark night of the soul.

The Christian faith offers hope with the 'beacon' of the risen Lord. There isn't any sense of whistling in the dark when our journey leads through valleys of the shadow. The key verse zeroes in on the wonder of the happy hope of our Lord's return. When this happens it will fulfil the many promises stated in the Bible. Until that takes place, we are involved in a waiting game.

Our Lord does not expect us to mentally, morally or spiritually hibernate as we wait. The exact opposite expectation is placed upon our shoulders. God's grace teaches us how we are to be active and involved as believers in an unbelieving world. Waiting is so demanding. Over and over again God's people are told about God's purposes and intentions. Next comes 'wait'! How were they to do it? By doing what they had to do as an act of service to the Lord. Unless we feed our hope of the Lord's return our capacity to wait will gradually be eroded. We will succumb to the scoffing of unbelievers. We will be silent with our testimony. Therefore, how do we feed our hope?

The most graphic answer to this must come from the book of Lamentations. This was written by Jeremiah after the utter devastation of Jerusalem by Nebuchadnezzar's army. The prophet penned words that break through the rubble and light a fire of hope in the heart. His words are stained by tears. The pathos of the book comes from a broken heart. As he sat among the ruins, despair must have been prancing before his mind, taunting and haunting him.

In Lamentations 3:19–26 we read his desperate attempt to hold onto Yahweh's eternal covenant: 'The thought of my affliction and my homelessness is wormwood and gall! My soul continually thinks of it and is bowed down within me. But this I call to mind, and therefore I have hope: The steadfast love of the Lord never ceases, His mercies never come to an end; they are new every morning; great is Your faithfulness. "The Lord is my portion" says my soul, "therefore I will hope in Him." The Lord is good to those who wait for Him, to the soul that seeks Him. It is good that one should wait quietly for the salvation of the Lord.'

Was Jeremiah happy? Not in the sense of laughter and frivolity. In the midst of overwhelming sorrow and tragedy however, he hoped in the faithfulness of God. Nor was his hope extinguished.

On what was it based? He knew the Lord as the God of Abraham, Isaac and Jacob who kept His promises. Jeremiah understood the Messiah had to come through the nation of Israel. This had not happened in Jeremiah's day. Therefore, the nation would endure. Yahweh's word and faithfulness made his hope blaze. Within that fire the prophet knew the glow of an inner peace and happiness.

Any sensitive person looking upon the world scene today would despair of better times ever coming again. Hope shrivels without a conviction that the world's events are pushing us ever closer to the Lord's return. God in His holy Word offers us hope. The more we feed this hope the greater will be its flame within.

Today's signpost: 'May the God of hope fill you with all joy and peace in believing, so that you may abound in hope by the power of the Holy Spirit.' (Romans 15:13)

Death Confronts Happiness
Day: 30

Key verse: 'I heard a voice from heaven saying, "Write this: Blessed are the dead who from now on die in the Lord." Yes," says the Spirit, "they will rest from their labours, for their deeds follow them."' (Revelation 14:13)

Unwelcome as death is, its presence and reality cannot be denied. Born through Adam's treason it haunts all of creation and justly deserves its title 'the last enemy'. (1 Corinthians 15:26) Happiness must look at death and stare it down. This is especially true for those living in harsh and oppressive circumstances.

Through John, the Holy Spirit has given us a glimpse of the most violent period in history—the time of the antichrist. It has yet to come. If believers in Christ Jesus are sustained during such a time, and the book says they will be, surely we can take heart.

Blessed are the dead who die in the Lord.

Once again we are told that happiness is location. We all must die. Unfortunately, not all die in the Lord. People have the choice to accept or reject, but they can't select the repercussions of their choices.

There can be no hope, no happiness and no heaven outside of Christ Jesus. How do we find ourselves 'in Christ?' 1 John 5:11–13 informs us: 'This is the testimony: God gave us eternal life, and this life is in His Son. Whoever has the Son has life ... I write these things to you who believe in the name of the Son of God, so that you may know that you have eternal life.' Faith isn't mere assent, nor is it passive. It is motivational. We hear and believe the Gospel which compels us to call out to Jesus as Saviour.

The apostle Paul's final letter sums up the confidence underlying happiness. He was waiting Caesar's execution order. In his writing there isn't any sense of regret. Caesar's sword would fall. Paul's spirit would rise. Such confidence still vibrates with a believer's triumph over death. The apostle was going into the presence of the Lord before Christ's return. Be encouraged, he wrote to Timothy, the Lord will return. When it happens there will be a crowning ceremony for all of the Lord's people (2 Timothy 4:7–8).

They will rest from their labours.

The word 'labours' is a picture of hard, wearying toil. In Revelation it also has the added stress of enduring the hatred of a godless regime. Through it all, the disciples have kept the faith.

Down the centuries many of Christ's followers have had a foretaste of the tribulation. Such men and women are sources of inspiration for us today. Together, we will share in the promised rest provided by our Lord. The meaning behind the word 'rest' points to refreshment. They are entering into the heavenly understanding of the Sabbath. This is a time not of idleness but of enjoying the favour of God and the pleasure of serving Him.

In Revelation 15 is a magnificent scene associated with those who have died under unpleasant circumstances. Their faith has made them victorious. God gave them a song accompanied by harp playing. This heavenly choir will stand around the throne and God will listen to their victory anthem. What a joy it will be to sing to the Lord God Almighty words He composed.

Their deeds will follow them.

We are saved by faith. We are rewarded by faithfulness. It isn't what we do for the Lord that earns His praise. It is doing His will in the power of the Holy Spirit. Rewards express the grace of God for our obedience, not our achievements.

As John watched the drama of God's people in the future, he detailed the coming hardships. In fact, he and others had a foretaste of those coming days. Yet he could still record that the happiness they had known because of Christ would not be crushed by persecution and death.

Faith in Jesus Christ gives us spiritual eyes to see beyond the shroud of death. We glimpse our eternal fellowship with Christ Jesus. Eternal happiness is to die in the Lord and rest from our labours. How sweet will be the tasting of such happiness!

Today's signpost: 'I am convinced that neither death, nor life, nor angels, nor rulers, nor things present, nor things to come, nor powers, nor height, nor depth, nor anything else in all creation, will be able to separate us from the love of God in Christ Jesus our Lord.' (Romans 8:38–39)

Those Whom the Lord Serves
Day: 31

Key verse: 'Blessed are those slaves whom his master finds alert when he comes.' (Luke 12:37)

Marriage features strongly in Jesus' parables. To understand them we must have an appreciation of Middle Eastern customs. We can read about the ten virgins in Matthew 25 and the wedding banquet in Matthew 22. Jesus Himself is likened to the Bridegroom who goes and prepares a place for His bride. His promise is to return when the arrangements have been completed. (John 14:1–3)

Part of the wedding experience was uncertainty. The groom's responsibility included completing the living quarters for himself and his bride. How long this took determined the extent of time before he could go to claim his betrothed. You can understand why this is an apt metaphor for the longed-for return of Christ Jesus.

In Luke 12 the focus is changed from the groom and bride. The centre of interest revolves around the servants. Perhaps the most astounding reference is to the master of the house. It is said he will honour the faithful servant. The master does this by becoming a servant to the servant. Such an honour is bound up in faithful service.

The theme of the parable is to create a sense of expectancy. Luke 12:35 resonates with this: 'be dressed for action and have your lamps lit'. The clothing in the Middle East is a flowing robe. This could be a hindrance when doing various chores. The servant, while doing the chores, would reach through his legs and bring the robe to the front. It would then either be tied to or tucked into his waist band.

How is this applicable for us today? Faithful service counts with the Lord Jesus Christ. Motivation for such work is a sense of privilege. Fuel to maintain an awareness of this honour comes from the storehouse of gratitude. In turn, such thankfulness keeps ears and eyes alert for the master's homecoming. The servants longs to see the master.

What undermines gratitude? Unbelief! What are the results? The parable portrayed it as a breakdown in moral and spiritual behaviour. Unbelief is a thief. It robs a person of integrity and an appreciation of the master's trust. Hardened, the soul creates an illusion of safety from judgement. Insolence would then breed a mindset which abuses privileges and people. In essence, such a servant is living as a pagan (Luke 12:29–30).

Years later John wrote to a church in Ephesus to encourage them. They faced mounting opposition. His words appear to vibrate under the influence of the parable: 'And now, little children, abide in Him, so that when He is revealed we may have confidence and not be put to shame before Him at His coming.' (1 John 2:28)

In the parable the servants are ordered to be dressed for service and to have lamps burning. You don't light lamps in the daytime. Therefore, the spiritual inference is that before the Master's return it will be a time of spiritual darkness. Those represented in the parable are to be 'lights' burning brightly. Here is the testimony to the expectant return of the Lord Jesus. In a darkened world this will not be popular but so, so, so necessary!

A torch needs a battery, a fire needs fuel and the Lord's servants need something to maintain their radiance. In 2 Corinthians 4:5–6 we read Christ's glory penetrates our heart through our knowledge of Him. It is as though we gaze into the face of the Lord when we read, study, hear or speak the Scriptures. Then we go about our daily lives reflecting His beauty in a non self–conscious manner.

Our quality of happiness is enriched by anticipation that our Master, the Lord Jesus Christ, will be pleased with us.

Today's signpost: 'Truly I tell you, he (the Master) will fasten his belt and have them sit down to eat, and he will come and serve them.' (Luke 12:37b)

The Search for Happiness

I climbed the mountain called Success
Surely there I'd find Happiness
Waiting to embrace my restless heart
And never, ever to depart.
Disappointed
I fell into the valley dark.

In the grottos of the valley's shadow
Pleasures called me, them to follow
Their masks such emptiness concealed
As passing time revealed!
Disillusioned
Elsewhere I must seek to be healed.

The solitude of the wilderness
Offered to my spirit happiness,
Self–denial, austerity the key
To feeling my soul's liberty!
Discouraged
Despair fed my deep misery.

On the city's street, up high
A notice, flashing, caught my eye
Happy is the man who trusts the Lord
Why not give Him a try?
Desperately
To the Lord Jesus I cried.

My search has ended successfully
Life can now be faced happily.
It comes, not from things, but from God
A relationship of faith and love
Deliberately
Found in the Christ of Calvary!

Raymond N Hawkins

www.ingramcontent.com/pod-product-compliance
Lightning Source LLC
Chambersburg PA
CBHW071030080526
44587CB00015B/2556